****

Here's is what people are saying...

Heart-felt praise for Celeste for writing this book about her own journey. It is full of inspiration, hope and encouragement for so many of us to become healthier, happier people. - *Judy Day, MAy, IYTT*

Celeste has encouraged, taught, me over the years to listen to my own body. To let my body and mind be engaged in who I am and have become. Our bodies are ours alone and through the journey that Celeste travels in her book, you will recognize how to become a person who truly loves how you look and feel. You will love the smile you wake up with everyday. *Victoria Shaw- Athlete*

Inspiring, motivating, revealing. Celeste reaches deep within herself as she reveals her journey to a healthier and fuller life. Celeste's words echo within me over the past 6 years that she has coached me and helped me develop a love for myself and my new gained level of fitness. *Debbie O'Connor -Athlete, Mother, Professional*

Celeste has a unique and precise ability to help me cut through my distractions, to find what's important to me at my core. She often reminds me I already have the answers inside of me. She has pointed out the tools I have, to recognize confidence, and clarify my path and find enjoyment in simplifying my life. *Suzanne Atkinson, MD*

Aware, Amazed, Share

The Truth Inside

Learning to Love and Trust Ourselves

from the Inside Out

Change your perception and you can change your Life!

Celeste St Pierre

Celeste St.Pierre
BA, Psych HHC

Published by Celeste St.Pierre 2014, Lincoln, NH

This book is not intended as a substitute for medical advice from a physician. The material contained in the *The Truth Inside:learning to love and trust ourselves from the inside out*, is for general information and the purpose of educating individuals on nutrition, lifestyle, health & fitness and related topics. Should you have any health care related questions, please consult with your physician or other qualified health care provider before embarking on a new treatment, diet, fitness or exercise program.

www.CelesteStPierre.com

Email: CelesteStPierre@gmail.com

All rights reserved. ISBN:1501045407
ISBN-13: 9781501045400

The Truth Inside

DEDICATION

This book is dedicated to all the "angels" in my life who have helped and supported me, and you probably don't even know it.

Thank you, you are all messengers.

CONTENTS

START..15

RECOGNIZE...18

Creating Awareness.. *18*

Internal Dialogue, Habitual Thoughts *20*

"I's" Have It: Owning the Experience *25*

Sameness of Being... *26*

Sameness of Being: Athletes *29*

Girls on Film... *31*

Mirror Effect... *35*

Hide the Scale *38*

Dissolving Structures.. *42*

Create Awareness with Meditation.................. *49*

Your Own Stories.. *50*

That's Too Bad You Feel That Way.................. *52*

Forgiveness *54*

What the Body Says for You............................... *56*

Intuition: Your Own Inner Guide.................... *58*

AFFIRMATION 60

    Turn It Around... *60*

    Creating Your Own Affirmation...................... *63*

    Gratitude Attitude.. *65*

    Today I Create My Life Experience *66*

    Non Judgement Day *66*

    Feng Shui Mind and Space *67*

    Writing... *69*

    Stop Drifting and Start Rowing!..................... *71*

    Laughter *73*

PHYSICAL... 75

    Movement Heals: Connect............................... *75*

    Lafayette campground 1993 .... *80*

    .... *80*

    Kona,Hawaii 2012.. *80*

    Resting, Ah Sleep!.. *81*

    Nothing's Gonna Stop Me Now........................ *83*

    Injury: Heed the Messenger *86*

    Bring Joy Into Your Sport *87*

    Being and Doing *89*

    Failure... *92*

    Mapping it Out.. *93*

Heart Rate *97*

Passing Health Along *106*

In the Name of Love! Part 1 .... *108*

FOOD 111

The Choices We Make *111*

What's good for us? *113*

Why Bother *116*

I'll Skip the "Syrup"—a true turning point .. *118*

How We Eat *120*

Athlete Eating *122*

Real Food *127*

Tired Eating *129*

I Eat What My Body Wants *130*

A Tip On Eating *133*

Nourish An Active Body *135*

A Binge is a Binge: Healthy Food Included. *138*

In the Name of Love! Part II *140*

Today I feel puffy *142*

Stillness Now *143*

Food: Mental Conflict *146*

Fear of Food *151*

Eating From the Heart *152*

EVOLUTION 154

Contrast *154*

The Sun Is Shining Wherever I Am *155*

Trust *155*

Confidence *157*

Oh, One More Thing *159*

ACKNOWLEDGEMENT

I am grateful for all my life experiences. Each person, situation, experience has been an "angel" sending messages to guide me along my path. Though there were many challenges, I would not change any

of it—as they have all led me to here, now. As a result of all these experiences, this book is written with gratitude as an acknowledgement to each of these people which are far too many for me to mention. I will simply say that if I have met you, then I thank you and acknowledge you regardless of how long or short our connection was.

START

"Sometimes it is necessary to reteach a thing it's loveliness."
Galway Kinnel

If you don't have challenges around eating, exercising, and loving yourself, then this book may not mean much to you. But, if you have been denying yourself or punishing yourself or don't have a healthy, loving relationship with yourself—if you cannot eat without then exercising, or you exercise to eat, or exercise to then *deny yourself* nourishment—then this book may be of some value for you. It may act as a pointer toward your true self.

Starting in high school, I remember being unhappy about my weight. Until my mid-20s, I had lost, gained, lost, and gained weight, significant weight- up and down for over 10 years. At one point in my mid 20s, I had gone to the local health clinic for a checkup. At Keene State college, just after high school, I met and made friends with a fellow student who was in the nursing program there. Ten years later, I went to the local health clinic for a check-up. Wouldn't you know it? She was now working at the clinic. I remember the shock on her face when she saw me there. In college I taught aerobics and ran every day. I was thin then; it was during one of my "skinny years". And now, I had puffed up to 212 lbs. She was awkward in seeing *this* body, I was oblivious and chatty, thrilled to see her.

I equate the years in my mid to late twenties to living under a bridge. It seemed I was at such a low point that my life couldn't be any more challenging. I was overweight, living at home in one of my family's apartments, waitressing, and not loving myself at all.

I would peruse the newspapers for work that was more interesting than waitressing. I found a newspaper ad looking for large-size athletic women to model active wear. Cool, I thought. That's for me! I enthusiastically went for an interview. The interview went well; they were excited and so was I!

Unfortunately, they said, I was not big enough!!

Not big enough! What? Rejected Again!

But as bad as I felt, it did open me a little to look at myself a bit deeper, though briefly. *Maybe I am not as fat and horrible as I think.* I saw a hint of my true self.

This book is me. But it is also you. In telling my story of being, I hope to inspire you to remember who you are, who we all are. My words act as pointers, not absolutes. My suffering has lead me to remembering my true self, hidden under layers of doubt and insecurity, judgement. Inspire you to remember the beautiful, amazing being that you are, too!

As I look back at the evolution of my life, I now can see it as a gentle process rather than a jump from that unhappy girl to the person I am today. I continue to open up a little more each day. I see each day as a opportunity to chose A or B, love or not love. To see life as it really is.

You have been inspired to pick up this book for a reason. As you read, promise yourself to give hope a loving chance, knowing that you, too, can walk through the door to your true self.

Keep getting up, taking steps each day to loving yourself unconditionally, until you get through the door to remembering who you truly are -Love!

The key is to *Love yourself*, not perfection.
Live Love!

RECOGNIZE

"A high degree of alertness is required. Be still.
Look.Listen. Be present".

Eckhart Tolle

Creating Awareness

Most people are not aware, awake, present, or truly paying attention. Ever. In today's world, many believe they can multitask. But not really. You cannot be truly present and actively noticing when you do many different things at one time. Yes, you *can* do many things at once; it's the *being present* to them all that you *cannot do*.

Doing an activity does not necessarily mean you are *aware* of what you are doing. You can do something mindlessly, or out of habit. Think about watching television while eating. You may be looking at the TV, while the hand habitually brings food to your mouth. But are you really present? That is, are you aware of taste, texture, fragrance, satisfaction of eating, in that moment? Have you ever looked down at your plate and wondered where all the food went—with no recollection of actually eating it?

First, awareness is paying attention to what you are thinking, saying, and doing and how it connects to *what you are getting* from the experience. Awareness rises as you begin to pay attention to, recognize, and fully notice your world around you, your body, your life. You become conscious of your decisions and actions, instead of your reactions. You make choices from a place of awareness. Making choices with awareness is the first step to uncovering your true self, joy—your true state of being.

We are all much more lovely and powerful than we think. We knew this as babies but, it got conditioned out of us as we grew and learned. As children, we are like precious gems moving through the world, looking at it with our own individual perspective, deciphering and trying to make sense of it. If we don't have someone we can trust to help us process the world, we put up protective walls to help us navigate and feel safe. Yet, to be the person we want to be,we have to take down the walls, so we can see the world as it is rather than how we believe it to be. Awareness is about *remembering* that we are all gems underneath the armor. This book is about reminding you. There is nothing new in this book that you don't already know. The key is to remember as you move through your day, to stay aware of, *to recognize the power within*. Our power is not outside of us as we have been lead to believe. Practice and live from the inside.

I speak of this unconscious living from my own experience. In my young adult years I was not paying attention to the world around me. I was self-absorbed with the thoughts in my head and my perception of life. I had no idea I could be, and actually was, in control of my own life experience. I had no concept that the way my life was turning out was of my own doing. In my case I was a victim of *not knowing;* I saw the world as I believed it to be, not as it was. I had no idea I could be and actually was, in control of my own experience. I had no concept that the way my life was turning out was of my own creation.

My thinking looped in a circle. From this unconscious state of mind, I saw the world as a place I didn't fit in, but one that judged me as "fat, unlovable, not worthy." I was agreeing with the world. The world was just reflecting back to me, me. Instead of knowing that my self-image was created by my own thinking, I fought my body, blamed it. I allowed myself to believe that the size and shape of my body was responsible for how I felt and thought and lived. The belief system I had, unconsciously, constructed to stay hidden in that world was that *if I could just lose weight, then I would have control over my own destiny.*

Of course that was a bunch of crap.

Internal Dialogue, Habitual Thoughts

We all have several thousand thoughts, or self-talk, each day, but generally we are not aware of them. These thoughts start as soon as we wake in the morning, and don't stop until we go to sleep again at night. It's an internal dialogue, it is incessant chatter! Pay attention. Be aware of it. Thinking is using the mind; *this chatter is the mind using us!* It includes the voices of others, as well as your past, habitual thoughts— programmed--thoughts. They very rarely, *to never*, serve us. Worry, fear, jealousy, pain, anger—to name a few—live here. Pay attention, notice: what's being thought and where does it come from? Whose voice is this? A teacher, a coach, the voice of your 8-year- old self ?

Awareness starts when you notice what you hear yourself thinking or saying frequently and habitually, including the cliches you tend to use.

This voice is *the ego voice.* I have come to think of and describe the ego voice is as the "passenger" in "my car." The car represents your body. The driver of the car represents your spirit essence, soul, or your true self. The ego passenger -your habitual thoughts and incessant chatter-is always, constantly, persistently *grabbing at the steering wheel,* wanting to take control.

Although we may not even be aware of the constant harangue of habitual thoughts, cliches, and chatter, these can form the basis of one's personal belief system. These thoughts often become, or form, our personal belief system or structure. Most people are not aware that this habituation is happening or has happened because it starts early and happens gradually. Thus, without even realizing it, we create structures and beliefs of our lives through our unconscious living.

Hence, Step One: Awareness.

This first step is only about noticing. I am suggesting here only to *pay attention* to your thoughts. Once you are aware of your habitual thoughts— that inner egoic voice—   you can decide if you want to make changes.

This does not suggest that you listen to every thought that passes through your mind, but do pay attention to *the repetitive, habituated ones*. It's also important to recognize that we experience what we habitually think about and focus on when we also attach great emotion to it. If you are thinking about "unhealthy, fat, tired, unlovable," and simultaneously feeling great fear and anxiety around these thoughts, *you* are feeding the experience of poor health, lack of energy, and not being loved. As your thoughts support the experience of *not enough*, your behavior follows in ways that support this thought, which is then followed by words that affirm *not enough*. Your body also responds to these thoughts, words, and behavior.

However, if you are happy with what you are getting in your life experience, then you will want to keep on as you are. If you want to alter what you are experiencing, first be aware of how your thoughts can create your experience. These beliefs and structures may be very deep in your consciousness, and therefore you never consider them and their affect on your life. You must bring them to consciousness before you can change your life.

As Gandhi said, "Keep your thoughts positive because your thoughts become your words, keep your words positive because your words become your behavior, keep your behavior positive because your behavior becomes your habits..."

Next, Step Two: Shifting Your Perception.

After you've become aware of your thoughts — your deeper beliefs and structures—start to create new thoughts that are in harmony with what you *do* want. You recognize what you *don't* want, so now think and say what you would like to experience. It's great fun once you make this connection.

I slowly came to this realization once I recognized *the connection between what I was getting and what I was thinking.* When I realized all my attention, all my focus and emotion was on "fat, looking fat, and feeling fat", then duh, "fat" is what I was always experiencing. It took me a long time to create new thoughts, my current thoughts were so deeply ingrained, so deeply habituated, but developing the awareness of my thinking allowed me to begin to be able to change.

This worked a little, a step in the right direction. I had to go further, deeper into this thinking, into these beliefs, Though I recognize that pain is part of life, my pain and suffering was really about avoiding the pain, pushing it down, away by focusing on being fat as the problem, but being fat was my identity. If I did change, permanently, who would I be? What I didn't understand through all of those early years was that the problem was being created by me as I attempted to escape the pain. Pain and bliss are part of life. They come and they go, so give them space to be known, to be felt, to be lived, let them have their say, then let them go.

At this point, I was better at connecting the dots. Only when I became aware of what I didn't want and learned that I could create what I did want— and still do; that is, to *feel* good—could I begin to experience it. Freedom is gained with a shift in perception. But was I worthy of it?

The next step in this process was to become aware of my beliefs. What did I believe about life, about my life, and about what was supposed to happen? I clearly saw that my belief about adulthood meant that I would "arrive," and once I did, everything would be perfect; and that perfection was connected to being thin—like being thin was a magical destinations that represented bliss. It would be a world where I would never be unhappy, there would be no pain, only kind words, and no one would ever hurt me. I would never feel small, or vulnerable. I would be safe from the challenges of the world, forever. There must have been something wrong with me, because I couldn't get there. Everyone else appeared to have made it, but I just couldn't get myself together to ever feel as though I had "arrived."

"I's" Have It: Owning the Experience

The best way to own your own personal life experience, which you have created, is by using *I* messages; that is, expressing your experiences using the word *I* instead of *you*.

One of my clients related a swim experience she had in the following way. "*You* know, when *you* round the corner of the swim buoy, and *you* come into the current, *you* are all confused and *you* can't see clearly which way to proceed. *You* just want to stop to get *your* bearings." Her story was expressed as though others, including me, all had the same experience. Not only can a conversation become confusing, but the impact of the story can easily be lost by inferring that the experience belongs to someone other than the speaker.

Replacing *you* with *I* would allow my client ownership of the experience, instead of generalizing it to include others, like myself, who were not even in the event. Using *I* messages, the story of *her* experience would read like this: "When *I* rounded the corner of the swim buoy, and *I* came into the current, *I* was all confused and *I* couldn't see clearly which way to proceed; *I* just wanted to stop to get *my* bearings."

Once you start to pay attention to your use of the word *I* to express yourself, you can to "own" your personal life experience. Begin by simply noticing your words. Are you recognizing that not everyone has the same experience as you? Are you referring to your own life experience as yours? As you develop this new awareness, you'll be taking an important step toward self-awareness .

You may need time to notice this habit of speech to catch yourself. Like everything, awareness is the first step of changing a pattern. Also, pay attention to those around you who are using *you* messages. Notice how it feels and sounds when they weave you into their experience which you had no part of. What do you notice and how is the message of the story being delivered? Is it confusing? Have you unwittingly done the same thing as narrator of your story?

My personal experience using *I* messages was challenging, yet powerful. I needed to have my own voice as part of taking control of my own destiny . The use of *I* messages allowed me to tell the world how I how felt about and experienced events, people, and places from my own perception. It told a more personal story: I am here, I exist, I matter, this is how I see it life.

Sameness of Being

God created us all equal in our capacity to create, to experience. We have free will. How amazing! We are all the same in our *being-ness* as humans be-ing, and we are free to create from our own human doing, the variety of which is evident by looking around at our world of abundance.

But what we do and who we are are not the same. Regardless of what I, or you, do or don't do, *we are enough*. We don't need to do anything to prove our worthiness. Yet we often silently, unconsciously, learned to tie our self worth to what we produce. Though each of us gets to choose how we experience our life through doing and perception—and we may not like what someone else does or does not choose— no person is more valuable or less valuable as a human being based on their doing or not doing, or what they have or have not produced, created, or achieved.

And yet we more often than not confuse this and perceive some people to be more important than others. They get to be more important in our culture, because we as a society believe that what they do is valuable rather than who they are—human. It can be challenging to see past the *doing* to the *spirit* in ourselves first, and then in others. But it can be done.

Start with creating the awareness that you are the same in your own "beingness" as those people around you, regardless of the *doing*. Do you feel or act differently depending on the company around you? Do you think of others as better than you or less than you? Are you not equals? Is the ego in you wanting you to be bigger or smaller? Or can you see your *sameness in your being* in all humans? Allowing that constant comparison of self with others either elevates or devalues both individuals. It separates us, not units us. We are all one.

Yet positive self-talk is often judged to be selfish, arrogant, or narcissistic. Or we feel silly and uncomfortable saying kind, loving things about ourself. Strangely though, it's okay to view others as "heroes." Why is it okay to look to others as better than us at the cost of our own self-worth? Why not strive to toot our own horn toward a healthy acknowledgement of personal talents, gifts, and passions? Why do we need or wait for others to do that for us?

I feel there is room for everyone to acknowledge their true selves, to expose their abilities, and to show we are all equal in our own being, our own unique greatness.

Look into your own eyes—the eyes behind the eyes, beyond the ego. Trying to look past your own ego can be like looking into a car with deeply tinted windows. The tint is like a "shell" of protection that makes it hard to see what is inside. This protective layer keeps out the sun, the light; it keeps others out. Pay attention, then look beyond the protection of the tint covering you. Looking past your own reflection in the tint to the driver inside the car —past the physical you—requires focus. This exercise is a pointer to who you — essence, pure potential.

So habituated is the ego connection in creating a layer of protection. This layer keeps out the sun, the light; it keeps true love out. Pay attention, then look beyond the protection of the tint covering you. You will then be able to see beyond others' layers of protection as well. We are all the same on the inside. As Anita Moorjani says so well, "To say that I hold another in higher regard than myself isn't real and means I am only performing." To *elevate* someone based on their *doing* means you must then consider yourself less.

Sameness of Being: Athletes

As "athletes", we step into the ring of competition nervous, hoping, wondering how it will go. We no longer see ourselves as equal in spirit to other athletes. To not see ourselves the same as others in spirit is to *place ourselves lower by elevating the others.* To judge ourselves or value ourselves by what we do, the outcome of our performance, is to say we are *less than others who have done more.*

We are not confident in our own ability to choose from our highest knowing in the moment of competition, our only true power is in the present moment, and we fear we will not be okay with the outcome, the finish line. We fear disappointment, and then beat ourselves up based on the outcome. We tie our self worth to the outcome,who we are is about performance results, not process. The fear can take many forms—that others may not love us given the outcome, or regret over decisions made during competition—but the true fear stems from not loving yourself unconditionally, regardless of the outcome.

Can you *love* yourself *regardless* of the outcome, regardless of how you finish the race?

These fears come from not knowing our true magnificent selves, not living in the present, conscious, moment, and allowing negative internal dialogue blind us to our own best interest. Again, this is about identifying who we are with what we do, affirming the belief that anything less than perfect means we are not enough. We fear not being enough. But, you *are* enough, regardless of what you do!

This is not to be confused with skills, fitness, or weight, or the physique, talent, or passion you may have; rather, it's about loving yourself on a spiritual level. This is about self-acceptance and appreciation, not self-judgment. Accept your current level of fitness, skill, and everything about your body, appreciating what you have or where you are now. Do not condemn nor judge yourself as less. The training you do is just that—something you do and not who you are. We are not our fitness, we are not our bodies, we are not our skills; we are much greater than that. Accept your current level of fitness. Be grateful.

I have read accounts, and heard stories from professional athletes about how they came to recognize their own being in their doing. Many of them found true joy when they let go of what they do and it's related outcomes, to embrace who they are: *a spiritual being doing an athletic event.* Success is not defined as making it to the podium. Success is being present as you do what you do. They have rediscovered their sameness of being.

Girls on Film

When I have looked at photos of myself over the years, I have not liked me in any of them. Does this sound familiar?

Usually I was looking at photos to see if I look fat, or how large I am in the pictures. How crazy and judgmental is that! Not a loving thought or action on my part at all. And yet, it's so habitual. I have done it and criticized myself so much for so many years, that it's a challenge to change. I know I am not alone in this.

Have you ever looked at a picture of yourself and did not like what you saw? The critical ego voice "turns on," perceiving everything which is "wrong" with your body, with you. The critical ego voice sees "flaws," like "fat" and all you see is "flaw," or "fat," and not the memory of the time in which the photo was taken.

The photo acts as a reminder of the body and all that is wrong with it. Many people with body image issues don't even want to have their picture taken, let alone look at the photo after.

For several years, upon seeing my picture, I would think: *If only I could be a little thinner, I would be a better athlete. I could run faster, I would feel more energetic, I would like myself—maybe even love myself!* I used to look at a picture and grimace, thinking: *If I could lose weight, my life would be better. Then, I would start to really live!* Exhausting, dramatic. When wearing distorted glasses, all one can see *is distorted.*

But then I became aware of something very interesting.

Over several months I had gained about 10 pounds. When I saw an old picture of myself again, back when I was 10 pounds lighter, suddenly instead of seeing me as "fat," as I did when I originally first saw the photo, I now saw that I looked good then, *thin.* I also remember being happier 10 pounds ago. If only I would have stayed at that weight, I lamented! I would be happy now! If only I could have kept the weight off, could get rid of these new 10 pounds, go back to the old me again, I'd be happy. Things would be different!

Eventually I caught on that I was just as miserable less 10 pounds or plus 10 pounds. I was so self-critical! I noticed that pictures of me at size 10 were terrible, until I was a size 14. At size 14, I saw how perfect I had been back then—at size 10. Oh, why didn't I see that then? If only I could've liked myself then. But of course, as many of you know, when I got back down to a size 10 *I still couldn't see it!* I still wasn't enough, I still wasn't happy; my life hadn't been miraculously transformed. I wasn't Cinderella.

However, my insight eventually became a step in the direction of liking myself—regardless of my size— as I gained awareness. What I became aware of was that it didn't matter what size I was, I just didn't like myself, my life. I just couldn't be happy. In hindsight, I wanted someone else's life.

This photo insight moment was enlightening. I have heard this with people who have anorexia. Their perception of themselves is that they see themselves as hideous and huge, even though they may be so thin their skeletal structure is exposed. We can see this, but they cannot. And yet they have no problems with their understanding of size; it's their *perception* that is skewed. So powerful is the ego mind to distort what it can.

My self-perception of me was like a game until I became aware of what was happening. The problem was that I didn't like myself, regardless. I was always critical, never good enough, could always be better. Because wherever I was, I was never satisfied. I noticed ultimately it didn't matter; I'd always be critical and unhappy. I'd never get there because I would never allow myself to be okay where I am now! No matter what, I did not accept myself. This awareness led me to the notion that I needed, wanted, to change my *thinking*. An aha moment, Bing, bing, bing!

For so many years I believed that changing my appearance would make me happy. Whether I was up 10-20-60 pounds or down 10-20-60 pounds, I was still not satisfied. Losing weight, changing my external appearance, did not make me happy. My habitual thinking was: *I still could stand to lose a little more weight, no matter what the scale tipped.* Or, I was fearful the weight would come back and my life would crumble, again.

My awareness grew. If I was critical now, and I was critical then, then it's not the weight that needs to change, not the external part of me—but the critical voice, the internal part of me. I can change that!

I saw this in myself over time. Each time I saw myself as fat in a photo, instead of agonizing over it, I would allow myself to be aware of the critical voice— to then question it, to challenge its validity, and to know that voice is the critical voice, *not my true self.* The critical, judgmental voice is a habitual tape that just pops up, like a song stuck in the head, on auto- repeat. I also wondered how my "seeing" could be so skewed, how could it be so situational?

I could have sworn on each first viewing of a photo that I was fat, chubby, or could stand to lose a few pounds. But as my awareness grew, as I practiced more loving thoughts, then went back to see the photo again, I was not any of those things. My kind, loving self-meter was developing.

Is anyone consciously taught to love himself or herself as they grow and learn? Not narcissism, but a healthy respect for the self ? I feel not. A majority of us didn't get the "it's okay to love yourself " memo.

It's not that the *photo* actually lies but our *perception* of it does. Our perception doesn't see accurately when coming from a place of fear, of non-love, the critical ego mind.

We see what we want to see and hear what we want to hear. My critical voice was just that, critical. Since I was living in a fearful negative-mind-made world, there was no room for anything else in my mind, in my perception, but criticism and judgment. That's what I saw, and that's what I heard.

When we come from a place of fear, that is to say judgment, jealousy, criticism, anger, and so on, non-loving thoughts and feelings, we will see the world that way. We see ourselves that way, not good enough. As I was judging and criticizing myself through my fear, my vision was skewed. It wasn't until I began to approach life from love, by *seeing myself first with loving eyes*, that I could then open the door to experiencing the world's joy, magic, amazement, and then sharing all of this. And with those same loving eyes to also see the world's pain, suffering, injustice, and it's contradictions then be able to sit with that discomfort of reality, not hide, ignore, or barricade myself from what is.

Mirror Effect

The world is our mirror. Th people, events, and things in our lives and the way we interpret them are reflections of how we view and explain our own world. You are seeing aspects of yourself in others, whether you view them in a favorable or in an unfavorable light. If what you are experiencing is upsetting or uncomfortable, this experience is reflecting back to you aspects you don't like about yourself, but not aware of in yourself, not willing to look at, or perhaps afraid of what you may find. It is helpful to remember that as you judge others, you are also judging yourself; and when you embrace that part of you that you don't like, you become more compassionate toward yourself as well as others.

The same is true of aspects that you do like in others. These situations are also reflecting back parts of yourself—those that you feel good about within yourself.

Because we humans tend to see the world in black or white—good or bad, like or dislike, want or don't want—we may be missing the gift when we push away, judge, or label anything, that which connects us, the real wholeness of what is. For some, it may be more challenging to see your beauty if you have been habituated to only see what you don't like. Others play small by elevating others at the cost of diminishing themselves. Still others recognize their wholeness, or at least the potential of living it. We are capable of both. We are not one or the other, but both.

Recognize when you are in mirror mode by paying attention to your thoughts, feelings, words, and your body. What might you be pushing away? Are you denying or accepting the current situation or the various aspects of yourself? Can you come to appreciate what is? When you experience this, when you catch yourself—laugh, laugh out loud! Welcome to being human. Your compassion meter has been turned up. Compassion for yourself rises up and overflows into compassion for others, "yes, I know, I can relate, I have been there." It connects us, we are connected. The shame you may have been carrying, the inflated ego, or the little-me ego is dissolving, and beyond this deeper unlimited freedom. Recognize that others are a mirror, a simple reflection of you.

During a conversation with one beautiful young mom I was working with, she shared an aha moment with me. For years this women had been so focused on, blinded by, her unhappiness with her own weight that she could not see her own beauty, her own magnificence. We had discussed the mirror effect, that others are a reflection of ourselves, at one point. Her aha moment came when a respected female family member had shared her personal dissatisfaction with her weight and lack of confidence in her own physical attractiveness. This client I was working with was in shock to hear this, and amazed that this family member could not recognize how beautiful she is!

My client suddenly saw herself in this woman. She observed and experienced it by hearing the critical voice in another, which is to say her own critical voice of this moment. *How are we so judgmental of ourselves, I of myself?* she thought. "This is what it looks like", she realized.

As I imagine giving others advice, what I would say to them, i stop or listen to myself, the thoughts—is this the message *I* need to hear? Is this more about me? Is this person reflecting back to me what I need to change or address in my life? Is this about what I am not conscious of? Usually it is.

Hide the Scale

In my own experience in addressing these issues of perception, here is what I learned and now I tell others. If you are weighing yourself daily, weekly, monthly, STOP! This was a huge step for me because I was *obsessed* with weighing myself. I allowed the number on the scale to determine how I would feel that day. If I liked the number on the scale then I'd have a "good day." If I didn't like the number, then I would not have a good day. I was allowing this contraption that simply showed me a number indicating the current weight of my body to determine how I was going to live my life, how I would perceive my day. Basically I was checking in to see if I was worthy of being here, of existing. All this from seeing the "wrong" number on a scale. It had never occurred to me to love myself unconditionally.

A sense of freedom slowly came with this realization. Not weighing myself was part of dissolving an old structure, an old belief as I tested it. Could I be trusted in this world? Would I be out of control? Blow up like a balloon and just never stop eating if I didn't weight myself? I stopped the compulsive weight checking, and lived through it. What happened is I began to trust myself, my body.

Consider these questions before stepping on the scale:

*What is my relationship with the current moment—what am I thinking, feeling, seeking?

*What will this number in the scale represent or tell me? What do I want it to tell me?

*How does my *body feel* before stepping on the scale?

*Who am I?

Now step on the scale. See the number. Ask yourself these questions while standing on the scale:

*What does this number say *to* me and what does it say *for* me? What does it represent?

*How does my *body feel* while standing on the scale? Is it now different than before seeing this number?

*Who am I as I stand on the scale looking at this number?

*Who will I be if this number was to change either up or down?

These questions are meant to give the scale watching some space so you can better understand your relationship to this compulsive behavior. What does this number mean for you: don't get to big, don't be seen or heard, I am small, I am a success, I am a failure, I am out of control, I am separate from this body, no one can tell me what to do, fuck all of you, I am worthy of existing, I am not worthy of existing? Does the scale bear testimony to whether you really exist or you are taking up more than your share of space? We want what we want, yet don't believe in our right to exist, based in this number. We don't believe we can have what we want, yet even when we have it, we don't think we deserve it. If you can gain insight from these inquiries and begin to understand your relationship with the scale, then you can begin to shift your perception and begin to live, seeing life as it is. Now.

And then there is the fear. If the number is the "right" number, the fear haunts you around keeping the weight off, to sustain it. For some, it is part of their identity. Would success at losing the weight mean that you would have no idea who you are anymore?

How can we meet ourselves where we really are and see the number just as a fact without attaching judgement and emotion to it? Notwithstanding a serious medical condition or the societal messages that bombard us about food and body image, the number doesn't really matter to anyone but the person standing on the scale. It's just a number. Can you see how your personal mindset and perception of it creates our individual, as well as collective, suffering? In the moment of suffering, come back to the now by letting go of the story you hold about what the number means. When we get caught up in one story, one mindset, we don't see that there can be more than one explanation for what we see. We easily forget that the body's conditions, including fluctuations in weight, vary from day to day depending on the variety of circumstances.

Instead of letting our perspective be ruled by an unconscious habitual mindset, come back to the present moment. Take a breath deep into the belly, feel toes, fingers, thighs, etc. Soften into the here and now. Feel the sensations, the aliveness within.

Earlier we discussed intentions. This is a great place to incorporate that practice. Be honest with yourself and look at the relationship with both desire to keep the scale as part of your habitual routine and to allow the number to rule your actions. The number *is* just a number. Without attaching meaning to it, it's just a piece of information that rises and falls like the temperature. Getting clear on what drives you to be a slave to the scale can change your perspective and bring a new feeling of freedom to your life. You can trust yourself, your body. You can feel the fear and still survive, by coming back to the now. By coming back to your body, the body you are in right now. Fear is a sign of time traveling- to being in the future or past, but not in the now where you can create and make conscious decisions. Use fear as an indicator to come back to your body, in the here-and-now moment of life. The hurt you have been burying, running from, hiding from has already happened. You don't have to go back, start here to let it dissolve. Fear can promote crazy behavior like bingeing, or starving the body by denying it food, or over exercising to burn off extra calories. We do crazy things for perfectly good reason. Our reactions may be crazy- what we do- but we are not crazy. We can take back our power we have been giving away.

See if you can dive deeper into your relationship with your desire to step on the scale by using the first few questions above. If you feel you must step on the scale, continue with the questions. These are just a suggestion to get you started with understanding your relationship with the desire, the scale, your body, your emotions, and who you think yourself to be. We are all brave and afraid at the same time. We don't need the scale to evaluate our worthiness to belong, we are all equally beautiful human beings. Punishment, force, or shame have no place here; they don't lead to love, self acceptance, kindness, forgiveness, patience, and understanding. You deserve it...because you exist.

Dissolving Structures

Structures form our belief system. These are the stories we have been taught, told, and believe, or formed on our own mind. And yet all structures are unstable; they are liquid, changing with us as we gain knowledge, grow wiser, and evolve. They are not a problem as long as we don't think of them as solid, stable, or never changing. It's those ideas and beliefs about how things are and how life is "supposed" to be that we over-identify with. Become aware of and recognize the structures in your world that you tightly cling to, and how your perception of them is causing you pain and suffering.

In adulthood, as I took steps toward healing myself from the inside, I discovered most of the pain and suffering I was experiencing was due to the beliefs—these structures—I had learned or created as a child and through my cumulative life experience. I was learning to question these structures, to test them, to experience for my self if they were true for me about how I thought I was supposed to live. To heal, I had to dissolve these structural beliefs.

As an example, I had to let go of my beliefs about the holidays or my "role" in the family. Birthdays, Christmas, Thanksgiving, Mother's Day, Father's Day, etc. The structure I created around these days was that we were to all be happy, celebrate and come together as one! Yeah! Sounds so lovely. But for me, it was not. I had given these holidays meaning and expectations based on my beliefs, and my experience always fell short.

I discovered I couldn't pretend to be happy when I was not. I felt like a fake, like I was playing a role on these holidays. I didn't feel it. In hindsight, I had anger in me, and I didn't want to be at my families home on that particular day. Celebrating was far from my mind. It took some time, but I eventually realized a holiday was just another day. It had no magic power, this day, but what I had given it.

It was during one particular Christmas with my family that I discovered on a very conscious level that I had expectations of myself and others. I thought I was "supposed" to behave or feel a certain way— happy, joyful, grateful—but I didn't feel those things. The day somehow felt different to me, but of course I was the one who was different. Yet, it was another day in the universe. What I found interesting, however, was that I could be there on December 26th and feel more at ease, more myself, more authentic. *How could this be?* I thought. Again the day was just another day in the universe, but to me it felt easier, less emotionally loaded than the day before.

I realized that what was happening was this: I was an adult doing my own thing out in the world, living my life, yet as soon as a designated holiday came, I became the little kid again, falling back into my place or my role within the family. It was as though I was an actress stepping onto the *holiday* stage. I was going to need time to dissolve my learned, habitual role, to break down this old structure. *To step off the stage.*

Again it took time; it took getting in touch with that inner build-up of stuff to figure out what was going on. Why did I fall back? I had to get in touch with those feelings stuffed down from when I was a little kid.

I would need to dissolve this structure I had created around holidays, and family, and look at my own role and my own beliefs around the holidays, events, family, and just going to my childhood home. It was my thinking, my perception, my expectations that all together were creating my unhappiness. I had to deconstruct all this stuff to see clearly what I was currently feeling in the now—to act instead of *react*.

I ask you to look at your own structures, your own beliefs about the world, relationships, yourself, marriage, roles, and so on. Once you have become aware of them, start to question them. Can you let go of certain beliefs about them? Does letting go of these structures/beliefs/stories offer more freedom, getting you closer to your true self ? Do they serve you to hang on to them? Are they at the core of your emotional suffering? Are you living as you think you are "supposed" to, or according to your own inner beliefs?

Low Fat, The Snackwell Era

I remember when Snackwell, fat-free snacks, came out in 1992. It was exciting to me because it was just what I was looking for: permission to eat an entire box of cookies. They gave me permission because they were fat free and fat in food was synonymous with fat on the body. My reasoning was I could eat the whole box and not get fat since there wasn't any fat in them, therefore I wouldn't get any more fat on my body.

It seemed to make sense as the American population, not just me, was starting to grow ever fatter. The culprit must be the fat we consume in our diets. Logic lead nutritionist and scientists to believe if we cut out the fat we ate we could stop getting fat as a whole nation. This makes sense but the body is much more complex than that, so we have learned since the late 1980's.

Dr Phil Maffetone wrote his book *In Fitness and in Health* in the mid 90's in response to what he was seeing with his patients. The ideas and suggestions in this book became a life changer for me. Most notable is the chapter "Fats Are Good For You!" This was the first time I'd ever heard this, and the way he explained it made a lot of sense. By following the suggestions in his book, my health started to improve. Some of my cravings and binges subsided with the addition of healthy fats into my diet along with reducing the simple carbohydrates and straight up sugar I was eating.

This idea of eating fats brought me back to the unquestioned structural beliefs I had had, in this case around foods that are high in fat. By trying the changes suggested by Dr Maffetone then stepping back to observe what happened in terms of how I felt, I was able to decide for myself what was right for my body. How do we know until we try, and how do we know unless we are paying attention. To our body. Not our mind.

The foods I started to consume that are high in healthy fats where avocados, olive oil, and nuts and seeds like almonds, sunflower and pumpkin. I ate whole fat yogurt, whole fat cheese, and real butter. Eggs from happy running around the farm chickens, and occasionally steak from cows that had been consuming a, mostly, grass diet. These were foods on my "don't go there list" in my mind. But when I let down my guard around these foods, I found I was okay. And I actually began to thrive.

Create Awareness with Meditation

Meditation is a chance to get quiet and still—to notice the ego voice, the internal dialogue, the chatter, the complaining entity. For me, it's like searching for the off switch in one of those big, dark Ikea warehouses. Meditation is a time to hear the constant chatter of the mind, then become transparent to it. Let it flow in, then out again, without grabbing onto it. Know the chatter is there, but don't give it any "air time." Instead, feel your body, notice your breathing. No need to sit for hours, knees crossed, though there is a place for that. One deep breath is all you need to come back to the body. Feel the lungs expand, the air flow in, then out again, deep, slow, calm, ease, notice the body; that's enough to wake you up, get you started or bring you back.

For some, this idea of meditation, or this level of paying attention, may be new and foreign. I remember the first few times of becoming attuned to my breathing and almost hyperventilating. It was a little scary. The sensation of my body, this awareness, of my own breath was so foreign to me. I felt I couldn't get any air, I couldn't relax, I coughed a lot. I was very disconnected from my body then. I calmly persevered, relaxed, and settled into it. What I would offer from what I experienced is to trust your body, which is to say, trust yourself. I trusted my body more than my thoughts.

There is tremendous value to sitting quietly. We don't do enough of it or never do it. We are always going somewhere in the mind, ahead of where we actually are. Start slow, one breath is a good start. Expand it gradually over time. Consider this a new lifelong practice, like brushing your teeth. It becomes part of your day.

The voice in the head will resist this idea of sitting quietly. Thoughts like: *Why bother? You have more important things to do. This doesn't work. Your mind/life is just too busy for this kinda stuff.* A little discipline is needed here to not react to this complaining entity. It's like a whining child in the background; know it's there, but there's no need to give it attention, that will only reinforce it. It will eventually tire and quiet down.

Before you start your meditation, you can ask yourself: Who am I? What do I want? How can I serve? Ask, don't answer; breathe, *feel* the answers don't *think* them. Tune in to your *pull* - your inner guide - it's sending you along your right path.

Your Own Stories

Awareness can arise by paying attention to the tales we tell ourselves and others. We repeat the same stories over and over, yet we may not even know it. Now with awareness, through meditation, by taking one deep breath, we can actually "hear" our own stories.

These stories are the ones that keep us stuck in our habitual patterns, connected to our structures, instead of our body, even though they may not be serving us any longer.

Listening to the same stories is like reading the same chapter of a book over and over. We never move on to the next chapter! Stories are carried forward from our past. Repeating the same stories, and believing them to be as rigid structures will keep us from having the space to make a new choice when the moment is ready for it. Letting go of structures can allow us to be more creative, try new things, and allow openness to the ebb and flow of life.

Once you have a connection to your thoughts, your story, you hear them. You see how the stories you tell yourself are creating what you are getting. You can now decide. You can begin to write of new experiences, instead of old stories. Move on to the next chapter, writing it as you live it. Each day is the start of the next chapter of your life. You get to begin creating new experiences that serve you.

Part of my old story that was keeping me stuck was that I was too fat, and that if I could lose weight, then I would be a much better athlete. This was merely an excuse, and part of my structure, that athletes are thin or lean or light. Clearly not so, as I was doing athletic things, such as running, swimming, biking, and hiking. I was also competing in races, and oftentimes, I was placing in my age category as well as winning a few of the smaller, local events. Yet, I could not see then how this old saga of mine was creating my dissatisfaction with my life. There was too much complaining of not good enough from the voice in my head to counter what I was experiencing. It's no different than the woman experiencing anorexia nervosa who cannot see herself as dangerously thin, so strong is the identification with that negative voice, the ego voice.

Once aware of how listening to my critical voice was creating unhappiness, I then could challenge it. "Was this thinking true?" My observation proved the answer to be typically "no." A shift occurred each time I questioned the validity of the critical voice.

That's Too Bad You Feel That Way

I was taught from a very young age that feelings and thoughts are either "good" or "bad." I learned not to say and think how I really experienced things. This *created much of my despair* from an early age. Instead of expressing myself honestly, and without fear of judgment, I used food to stuff down my feelings. Literally. Instead of getting them out, expressing them, actually *feeling them*, acknowledging them, I literally hid them away with food. I don't think of this as either good or bad, it's just what I did to survive, it was my method of surviving moments I didn't have any other tools to use. I had good reason to do what I did. It was the only thing, what else was I going to do? It took forever to de-condition this judgment and stop using food like tape over my mouth.

What I have come to recognize is that feelings and thoughts just are. We are neither our feelings nor our thoughts, though both are part of us, part of being human. Growing up, if I expressed some "bad" or "negative" feelings I was told, "That's too bad you feel that way." My takeaway was that I should not feel the way I do. There was pity and shame if I felt this way, and the message I received was that *I should not share my feelings*. Also, I must "be bad" if I felt a particular way. Not that the feeling was "bad", but that I somehow was "bad." Very confusing, but a powerful set of messages.

Are you pushing away the "bad," your "dark" side, what we call negative? We cannot only embrace our "light" or our "positive" side. We also need to acknowledge the parts of ourselves we may not like or want to acknowledge. To be human is to embrace and accept all of ourselves, to love ourselves unconditionally, not just under certain conditions. We want it both ways, when we do something great we want it to be about us and when we don't do something great we want it to be about something outside of ourselves.

This means acknowledging the dark— what we may

not like— along with the light—the parts of ourselves we do like. Though we cannot always be positive in our thinking, speaking, and doing, we never get it wrong either. Life just is. We can choose our thoughts and feelings without judging them.

Loving ourselves means loving ourselves, even though we may not say the right or perfect thing. We love ourselves, even though we may have negative thoughts about ourselves or someone else. We love ourselves even though we may have just yelled or honked or sworn under our breath at someone for cutting us off in traffic. Or yelled at our children or partner.

We don't just love ourselves when we do a kind act, or use kind loving words. We embrace all of our human feelings. Feelings don't need to be judged, just acknowledged with kindness. We learn from both the "good" and the "bad" and move on along our path.

Forgiveness

For many years I thought forgiveness was a good thing and necessary thing to do in an effort to heal myself. To forgive myself for things I had done, people I may have hurt, things I may have said, and to forgive others for the things they did that hurt me. Healing seemed to start by forgiving myself, first, then forgiving those people who had angered or hurt me. But anger or hurt was my perception of the situation or person. I have come to learn that I did the best I could at the time, given my level of awareness. I have come to recognize that what I did or said that was hurtful came from a place of anger and fear, and not love and awareness.

Forgiveness, according to Anita Moorjani, is saying, "You were wrong, you hurt me—and even though you did something wrong, I will still forgive you." I can appreciate this explanation.

Yet it has always been up to me to decide how I want to interpret the situation. I can choose to feel the hurt and anger, and in the past, that's what I chose. But I have come to understand that I did what I did (or they did what they did or said) from a certain level of consciousness, or unconsciousness, *in the moment*. That is, either I or they did the best we could in that moment. If your unconscious, you don't know your unconscious to be able too act consciously. I couldn't have acted from conscious love, because I didn't know! So I reacted from unconscious fear. I see this now. Now I have a choice. Now I can choose to act from my place of conscious love, or react from my place of unconscious fear.

If I forgive myself for past actions, I would be saying, "I did something *wrong*." But instead, if I can look at my world without judgment of right or wrong and see we are all making choices from our present level of awareness, then there is no right or wrong—only *what is*. This is the same as feeling either good or bad. We are all creating our own experience, and we create from our present level of consciousness or awareness.

Instead of forgiveness being based on wrongdoing, "You wronged me or I wronged myself," you can shift your thinking, "I will *let it go, surrender to what happened.*"

Then there is no need to forgive, just to understand the consequences of the outcome when coming from a position of fear. "Forgive them, for they know not what they do," said Jesus. They did the best they could from what they knew.

What the Body Says for You

The body is a messenger. Recognize how your body has been serving you. When I found myself emotionally eating, I had to look and see how my eating *when not hungry* had been serving me. I find everyone's story is different. What does your body, or fat, say or not say for you? What does the food provide or not provide for you? At one point I came to see that I couldn't let my perception of my body go until I could recognize its gifts.

There has been a very good reason why you are eating past fullness, or why you deny yourself of food. There is a very valid reason that only you can sort out (you can always get support with this, but ultimately only you will "know"). You will want to put some energy into sorting this out. This is a good thought to take into meditation.

For me, eating acted as a protective barrier between me and getting emotionally injured. Eating soothed me, though temporarily, from emotional pain. I used food to stuff down my feelings, to avoid them, my true feelings about things that I was taught were wrong or bad to think or feel. Because I learned my feelings were bad or wrong, I thought if anyone knew my true thoughts, they wouldn't like me, love me. I would be rejected if people, the world, whomever, really knew this about me. I would be alone. So I stuffed this down—being the bad person I thought I was—I thought I would be protecting myself from rejection. I had also confused my feelings as me instead of something fluid that comes and goes.

I focused my energy on my body, my weight, my fat, to save me from the voices of a deeper fear —not standing up for myself, not speaking my truth, not saying what I wanted, loneliness, not getting what I wanted/needed, feeling guilty, not being lovable if people knew the truth about me, not expressing my anger, ultimately not loving myself unconditionally- all the monsters that et rolled up in the belief of not being enough.

On one hand, my eating was about self-loathing. On the other, it was about padding me, a buffer zone of protection and safety. It soothed me, even if only temporarily. When I could or would face this, and it took some time to slowly un-stuff all that I had stuffed down, that's when my life began to shift. I would learn to love all of me, both the so called positive and negative feelings. I could not reject or ignore any of it. All of it is in me.

Make time to consider how the weight, or your discontent for your body, is helping or supporting you. Does your weight pad you as mine did? Does your weight protect you from the past? Is this self-sabotage because you think you don't deserve to be happy? Are you stuck in your story that you didn't get enough somewhere along your path, *the weight keeps you full?* Do you want it to provide a protective safety barrier between you and life?

Intuition: Your Own Inner Guide

Listen to your own inner voice to guide you. Though it's not really a voice, it's the tug or pull to move in a certain direction. Your highest first thought. It's the thought that encourages action to follow an idea before the ego voice latches on. There is the inner pull of guidance, your intuition or the ego Voice of distraction.

One afternoon, I was heading out the door to go to the post office when I had the thought pop up to take my umbrella with me for the walk. It was an impulse to take it, but then the ego voice came in, "Don't bother, it'll be fine. You don't need that. If it rains you'll just get wet; you'll live." So I ignored this little tug and instead listened to the seemingly logical inner critic. As you can imagine, it poured rain and I was soaked. As it was pouring down on me, I was certainly wishing I had that umbrella!

Intuition or inner guidance can come from within, an impulse or tug, or from the external such as overhearing a conversation or reading something in a magazine, that catches your attention. Your inner guide picks up on these "hints" to move you in your best direction or to keep you on your path to what you want or have intended. Sometimes it may not make sense, but follow it. It may lead you to your desired destiny. You don't have to see the whole path, simply trust. You will know if you are on your path, as things will seem to fall into place. You will experience love, ease, flow. It will unfold, you won't have to chase or hustle. There is action on your part, but ease occurs as you heed the message from your inner guide—from love.

AFFIRMATION

"Our deepest fear is not that we are inadequate.
Our deepest is that we are powerful beyond measure."
Marianne Williamson

Turn It Around

I love affirmations! I smile when I read them, which is the point! You can turn your old habitual thinking, which is not serving you, into affirmations. An affirmation is a strong positive statement expressed as though something is already so. By becoming aware of what your beliefs are, what you are currently thinking, speaking, and then acting on, you can then choose if what you are getting is what you are wanting.

You can decide if this is the experience you want to be having. If not, you can choose differently to create a new experience.

Most of us, prior to awareness, probably have been affirming what we don't want, and as a result— getting that. You are likely familiar with the phrase "be careful what you ask for, you just might get it." I have heard this but it's always been in a negative context; be careful what I ask for, I just might get something I *don't* want.

It never occurred to me to ask for what I *do* want. Many of us are more familiar with what we don't want, so much so it's awkward to consider what we would *like* to experience. We fear being disappointed if it doesn't come, so we play it safe keeping expectations low. Most of us aim too low.

Once you realize what stories you have been believing, thinking and speaking of, and then acting out, you can start to turn them around.

Start by writing down one habitual thought that you have become aware of that you want to change. Then write your new statement, or affirmation, as though you have reached it. Athletes have been using this for years, by saying what they want as though they have it—and then visualizing it being done, plus attaching strong positive emotion to having it, and then acting it out in training.

Affirmations offer a process to create what you want to create, then align your actions with it.

The affirmations we choose with awareness create what we then do. When faced with a choice, reflect on the affirmation to serve as a guide. The affirmation already supports our actions. Our actions start with conscious thought; we use thoughts to act instead of react.

Begin to turn your life in the direction you want by choosing affirmations that support what you want. Turning your life experience in your right direction starts with understanding your deeper beliefs and testing their validity, then thinking and speaking about what you want, not what you don't want.

Then live as though it is already so.

It has taken me a long time to get this. I have carried with me for as long as I can remember—having learned it from my family, who likely learned from their parents—the story of never having enough. Enough of anything, food, time, money, kindness, love, etc.

I wanted to turn the story of not enough into something that would serve me. My thoughts had been around "not enough," and I frequently heard myself voicing those thoughts. For example, I was very good at spending the money I did have, which then left me with very little, not enough, money. No surprise. I was acting from my beliefs, thoughts and words of not enough, so that is what I experienced. However, it was apparent that I did have money given my travel, clothes, cars, bikes, furniture, etc. I didn't have cash, but I did have "stuff." And again no surprise, I didn't think I had enough stuff.

The way I turned this around was to first realize my deeper belief of not enough. I became aware just after I said or thought "not enough." Then I would catch myself in the midst of saying not enough. Eventually, I was able to stop myself from believing, thinking or saying anything contrary to what I wanted to experience. When it came to money, I reflected on the things I owned, my travels, my savings. I must have enough, look at all I have done, and own. Enough isn't quantifiable, so how would I ever have enough.

One key in this evolution was to not to judge myself any time I noticed doing this and allowing myself to learn acceptance. I didn't need another reason to judge or criticize myself for not being good at turning things around. Through this process, each time I caught myself saying "I don't have enough," I would immediately think and sometimes say aloud with great gusto, "I have more than enough, I am more than enough."

Creating Your Own Affirmation

Write down what you want to experience. If you're not sure what you want, then write down what you don't want. Let's use "I *don't* want to eat sugar every day" as an example of what you *don't* want. So turn this old affirmation around by stating what you *do* want to eat. If you don't want sugar, then what would you prefer to eat? You may want to eat a variety of colorful, fresh, unprocessed foods that feel good in your body and give you energy.   So your affirmation could be: "I choose flavorful, fresh, and colorful, foods that feel good in my body." It is stated in the positive, and it is what you want to experience.

Next is to make time in every day imagining and visualizing these foods, eating them, experiencing the taste, flavor, color, and smells in your mind. Feel, imagine, and pretend as though it is so. Then let it go. As you do this with strong joy, you are more likely to find yourself in the produce section of the grocery store than in the ice cream aisle. Because you have done this work, you will likely choose foods that are in harmony with your thoughts and words.

Take an old story, recognize how it is keeping you stuck, consider what you do want to experience, create an affirmation by positively stating what you want—as though you already have it. Then let your emotions and imagination embrace this!

As you do this at first, as you practice this, I ask you to start with a single-minded focus. Start with one affirmation at a time to give it more oomph! It's like going to the gym, building slowly, gradually to develop your creativity muscle.

You may feel silly at first and that's okay. You want a silly, fun, playful approach. It may be unfamiliar at first, and you may not believe it. But stick with it, trust, don't look under rocks for what you ask for, just let it find its way to you. Just be aware of what you ask for, you have it.

Gratitude Attitude

Oh, how the ego does not like gratitude! Gratitude has the same effect on the ego as water did on the Wicked Witch in the *Wizard of Oz* or like kryptonite to Superman. It weakens and dissolves the ego slowly. The more frequently you recognize and state how grateful you are for all that you have, no matter how big or small, the quieter the egoic voice becomes. Take time each day to acknowledge all you have to be grateful for. Now. In this moment.

You could make time to write your personal gratitudes out. Get a notebook to create your own "gratitude journal." Spend a little time in it each day, noting 10 things—people, places, events, books, nature, anything, anything at all—that you are truly grateful for. Start with being grateful for your breath if nothing comes to mind, or be grateful for having clean drinking water.

As you practice, the momentum will come snowballing down on all of those things that you already have to be grateful for. You will begin to notice how full and rich your life *already* truly is, now! I enjoy making time in my day to write out 10 gratitudes. Gratitude enriches my life experience!

Today I Create My Life Experience

What a fantastic way to start your day, consciously choosing what you want to experience. This is a great exercise: *to write out what you wish to create in your experience.* It's so easy to let the day happen with a series of reactions to what happens. But, with this new practice, you set your intention as to what you choose to experience. You can, for example, create the experience of perfect health, even if it lasts only a few minutes, or seconds!

Recognize what you are experiencing now and know that you created it. You can appreciate it or you can change it. With paper in hand start with "today I experience..." "Today I experience ease and flow as I move through this world." Take time to write it out. You can revisit this at the end of your day. What did you experience? Did it coincide with your intentions for this day? Have fun with it. You get to create your life experience, so this is an opportunity to put it out there, step back...allow it to unfold.

Non Judgement Day

Today *I judge no thing, especially myself.* You may not recognize that you are judging yourself, but if you judge yourself, you are also judging others. Deep, lasting, true change starts from within. Love starts from within, which means accepting yourself. See if you can have a day without judging.

Look at things, events, and people as neither "good" nor "bad," but instead see everything as just "is." I am not saying you have to like or enjoy, but to allow without the label of good or bad. It is what it is. Accepting it, whatever it is, then proceeding from there.

You may be in tune with judging big or obvious things, but how about the little judgements on yourself or others? Do you...have *sadness* or *anger* in you after eating a box of cookies, or not completing a training run fast enough? Or think you are *stupid* because of the way you handled a work situation? Dislike the person who *stole your* parking space?

When I recognize myself reacting by judging myself or others, I laugh! My laughing diminishes the ego. I am human, so I let go of judgement as soon as I recognize it as such.

Starting with little things in your day, see if you can let go of the judgment that what you did or said was this or that. Peel the label of either "good" or "bad" off. This non-judgment practice is one big, yet tiny, step to self-acceptance, to self-love.

Feng Shui Mind and Space

Feng Shui is the ancient Chinese art of placement to promote the harmonious flow of energy in a given space. Clearing the clutter in the home improves the flow of energy in all other aspects of your life, such as with prosperity, personal success, and health. Who doesn't want that! Begin with clearing the clutter of the home and the mind.

Start with the mind. Get clear. Open up the mind to move the clutter, the unsupportive thoughts, out. Keep the thoughts that are serving you; let go of the thoughts that are not. What thoughts have you now become aware of that you can let go? Not to ignore these thoughts, but to notice what is helping, supporting your true self- love- and what may be blocking it. Practice this simple exercise. Whenever you notice stress or anxiety in you, or feeling disconnected from the body, take one deep breath. By doing this, you use the breath to bring you back to yourself, to clear the clutter from the inside so you may make choices more in harmony with the flow of life.

In your home, start with one area that is really bugging you. Ask yourself: what can I give away, what needs a new home of its own, and what can be recycled or tossed? Sometimes it is hard to let go of stuff, especially if someone gave it to you. Keep in mind the person is not the item. Take a moment to remember the person that gave you the item, thank them in your mind, bless them, and then find someone else who could use and appreciate the item, then gladly pass it on to them.

I apply this practice of clearing the clutter in my own home frequently, especially when I feel overwhelmed or stuck. It is amazing to do, it really does get the energy flowing again. Moving the stuff in my home helps me move the stuff in my mind. By simply cleaning the clutter from my home, I also open the flow of energy, which allows more ease in me. *I* opened up! Interesting. Fun things come my way after I move physical stuff out. Give it a try and see what happens!

Writing

I love to write! We are all writers. It's a fabulous! It is also a fantastic way to get clear, practice self expression, be creative, and become aware of the critical voice. It is a way to sort things out. There is no need to think about the quality of your writing, just write for yourself, for your own wellbeing.

Writing is another opportunity to let go of self-judgment, too. I make time almost everyday to write in a notebook. My earlier journals were about being a victim in my own life, yet they have evolved with me.more than that, they have *helped* me evolve. Back then, little did I know then that I was in control of creating my own experience. The writing helped me move through my victim role and get out of it. When I look back in those journals, though, they are not all doom and gloom. There were some tiny threads, glimmers of wanting a better life. I wrote to help myself.

"In a thousand little ways the writing keeps me from abandoning myself." Julia Cameron from *The Right to Write*

Writing was a way to figure myself and my life out. As helpless as I thought I was then, I have always really wanted to do things on my own. This drive for self-reliance—my deep underlying desire of "I can do it myself"—in my writing quite regularly.

I encourage you to make time in each day, or a few days each week, to quietly sit with the intention of writing out on paper the chatter going on in your mind. Listen, and write. This is a great practice in paying for attention to the voice in your head. Notice it and creat space for an awareness around it.

You may find that as you write, you get past the chatter and your mind settles in a little. Interesting things then have room to come up. Suddenly you are aware of the beauty, the stillness, the scenery around you!

Keep in mind that your writing is not about creating a novel or whether it's "good." Rather, it's a chance to give your thoughts a tangible form; it's also a means of noticing the constant loop of repetitive thoughts that keep you stuck. Writing is an opportunity to get in touch with the shenanigans of the mind, to sift through and to help you get clear to what's really going on. Think of it as a deep, inner Feng Shui to clear your slate each day. This is not the same as the gratitude journal, but an extension of it. This writing creates awareness of thoughts—habitual thoughts—before opening up to the deeper creative mind where solutions and answers to challenges can be heard.

Stop Drifting and Start Rowing!

Are you drifting around in your life by not consciously putting expressing what you want? Are you adrift, not steering but letting the wind blow you where it will?

Create a direction for your life. Consider that how you spend your days is how you live your life. What do you want? Write it out and work on it over the next six months to a year, if not more. Goals and intentions are like looking at a map. You say you want to go somewhere or experience something. This is about creating the steps to getting there.

Extending your practice of writing— getting clear, listening in on the mind, sensing the body during meditation—you are ready to write out some goals and/or intentions. Think of goals as being something measurable and visible to others. Intentions, which are not measurable, are personal, internal feelings you want to experience. Begin with three goals or intentions for the first month. Write out three more to accomplish at the end of the next three months, three more to finish at the end of six months, and three to achieve by the end of the year. Once you decide what they are, the practice of writing them adds power to them. Then,, review them each day, and keep the time frame connected to the goals. But don't make it about the goal, it's about the process, the steps you actually take that bring you to the goal. It's not that you achieve the goal but how you got there.

In my experience in working with women, this is where most women will list weight loss goals. This is fine, but keep in mind that the work starts from the inside, that is to say *loving the self under any condition*, which includes one's physical appearance and given weight at any moment.

If you make it about the weight—the number that shows up when you step on the scale—as opposed to feeling good, you might engage in crazy, unhealthy practices to lose weight.

I have set many goals to lose weight over the years, thinking I would like myself more and that my life would be better if I weighed less. I thought looking better would make me happy, and of course the love of my life would then appear and all would be complete. Then I would be complete. As though I wasn't enough already.

However, I lost weight only to gain it back. And, when I lost weight, I feared I *would* gain it back. My life never became perfect, and I certainly did not like myself more. I was still insecure, jealous, fearful—dependent on others for my sense of worth and joy, feeling needy and incomplete. I still felt small in the world, just as small as when I was physically big.

It was when I focused on health and becoming more fit, that the weight began to come off. What makes up my health is, meaningful work, kind friends, spirituality, meaningful relationships, and creativity to name a few. Only when I began to focus on these aspects that encompass all of my health, did the love and respect I needed begin to develop. Being physical, resting, nourishing myself with foods was part of my health. I was able to see my health in a bigger, broader more satisfying light.

My advice is to *skip the weight loss goals and begin with goals or intentions that will support feeling good*. A goal around feeling good may be to exercise three times a week by walking with a friend. This is external, measurable, and public. An intention that would support this goal is *to be accepting of the experience of walking, as it unfolds*. This is internal, not measurable, and personal. Another example of a goal is to meditate or sit quietly for 15 minutes, five times per week. An intention to support this is *to not judge the meditation practice, accept the experience as it is*. You can also use your goals or intentions and turn them into affirmations.

Make conscious choices to row your own boat, that is, lead your own life instead of drifting around. This *is* the big show.

Laughter

Never underestimate the power of a good laugh! Not to make fun of yourself, but watch funny movies, funny shows, and have fun with friends. Laugh at the absurdities in life. And there are always cat videos! Be sure not to take life too seriously, yet don't use humor or joking as a protective shell.

Instead, embrace all of your emotions, all of your feelings. They are part of you and your overall life experience. Embrace the joy and the healing power of laughter!

PHYSICAL

"A ship is safe in the harbor, but that's not what ships
are for."
-*William G.T. Shedd*

Movement Heals: Connect

I have been a Pilates instructor for several years.
During my training, *movement heals* was our motto. I
believe this with my whole heart. Intelligence resides in
every cell of the body, not only the cells of the brain. It
is *through* our bodies,in a combination of physical
activity and stillness, that we can connect with that
universal intelligence. We can do a great deal of healing
emotionally and physically with movement.

One great insight I had on my path to healing
myself was to use exercise to feel and express love for
my body, to move, and feel the aliveness within. Over
many years, I slowly shifted my exercise purpose *away
from the external* of using it to lose weight, gain muscle,
and look fit. I noticed I found *more enjoyment* using
exercise to get out of my head, use it as a moving
meditation and to experience nature. I discovered
appreciation and gratitude that I have a healthy and fit

body. I enjoyed exercise more when I stopped expecting the outcome of losing weight—and instead, simply did it for the joy of moving. Because of this approach, the training for racing was much easier, enjoyable, and I am still inspired to do it to this day.

What type of movement *moves you*? What do you feel pulled to do? Sit quietly, take a deep breathe to get in touch with the sensations in your body. What is it asking for? What does your body, not your mind, desire? The mind will want to be lazy, or it may want to do something more exciting than exercising. What type of "movement desires" stir from within you?

Move because you want to. Move because it feels good in the body to experience the sensation of muscles moving. Move as a symbol of love for your body—and not out of fear of becoming ill or fear of gaining weight if you don't.

Whatever answer comes is a pull, a desire, an inspiration from your deepest source. Moving is a way to connect with that source. You don't have to go to the gym to lift weights or walk on a treadmill, unless of course that is your desire. Expand your ideas of what physical activity is. Consider Zumba, Jazzercise, or ballroom dancing. There are so many options out there, I ask you to broaden your thoughts around movement.

Over the years, I have encouraged women to come to my fitness classes at the gym. Some do join, but surprisingly, many of them tell me they will attend *after they lose some weight.* Hello!

They are waiting for perfect. It's that same old story— told by the voice in the head— that once you lose weight, you will begin to live your life. But perfect will never come! Why wait! Start now!

Care for your body now by using movement as a way to show love and reverence for yourself. Get in touch with your inner athlete. You get to choose what you do, so have fun with it. You will never choose wrongly. Chose to do it out of love for yourself. You may need to let go of old stories. Movement will heal you, as it did me, and still does today. It will connect you to yourself, and all that is. It fills you up!

"Movement fills an empty heart." *Robert Fagan, PhD*

The key to whatever physical activity you undertake is this: use it as play time. Play around with the intention to connect with, not disconnect, from the body. I suggest that you skip the earphones while at play because they tend to serve as a distraction by keeping you in your mind, rather than attention on the physical. The egoic voice in the head doesn't want connection with the body, for fear that connection will diminish it. So it labels exercise as boring. You want to just get it over with. You want to be entertained, then reap the rewards of exercise without actually being there for it. Or maybe you're using exercise time to multi-task—

you are a busy, important person who has a lot to do. Who has time to exercise! Remember This is play time. I ask why disconnect at all? This is your life; be present in it!

Our bodies have so much valuable information, feedback, *to guide us*, along our best path! Use this time to listen to and connect the triad—mind and spirit with the body—to feel the body, to increase awareness of it. Hear its brilliant guiding messages so you can learn to trust it, again.

Feel the muscles working; they are like messengers to the aliveness within the body. Use this time to separate the egoic mind's desires from the body's desires. The body will hold the ultimate truth for you; you'll be guided by feelings and sensations in the body. This is where you will hear your deepest truth.

I ask you to exercise with the intention to stimulate the body, get the energy flowing, and to heighten your awareness of the sensations in the body. It can be a moving meditation. Exercising, like meditation, can be a chance to quiet the mind, tune in to the body, and get clear in thought. Not to look for a solution for a problem, but *to let the solution come to you*.

Focus on the movement, the now, without judgment. Hear the judgement, "I don't like this. When is this going to be over? This is soooo hard!" but continue to stay in the now, noticing and appreciating the physical sensations you are experiencing. Feel sensations, not think of labels that judge.

Heed your body's inner guidance. It will tell you things like when to rest, when to push, and when to be still. It can heal you both mentally and physically when you hear and listen to its messages.

Lafayette   campground
1993

Kona,Hawaii
2012

Resting, Ah Sleep!

Most important for our health, of course, is sleep; yet, it's most ignored as we push ourselves to do more. Doesn't everyone feel better after a good night's sleep! But when this doesn't happen, we tell ourselves that we live in a fast-paced world. That's our personal and cultural story; our self worth is tied to what we produce. So, we then perpetuate this view of things by staying *very busy*! However, sleep is a big part of our overall health picture. We all need to allow body, mind, and spirit to regenerate with rest and sleep.

I have learned that by getting quality sleep, I feel healthier overall. I have more energy and tend to eat less. I also now recognize that when I am tired, I eat more. I used to interpret my body's need for sleep as a need for more fuel. I would react to my body feeling tired by eating to bring my blood sugar up, when what I really needed was some shuteye.

When we don't allow ourselves to rejuvenate the body through rest, stays in a constant state of stress. Hormonal levels stay high in the "fight or flight" state. Thus, fat burning is turned off. Quality of sleep then goes down, and the next thing you know, you are on a downward spiral! Not enough sleep or rest means you eat more to bring the blood sugar up. But that doesn't work because low blood sugar is not what's making you sleepy. You are experiencing *tiredness* because *you are tired.* Coffee and caffeine in its various forms are not the solution. Getting sleep is.

I discovered when I allowed myself—that is, *gave myself permission*—to slow down and stop to get some rest, I lost weight and my hormonal levels balanced out once again, no drugs needed—just adequate sleep. My body came out of its perpetual state of stress. Hmmm…can I say I lost weight because of sleep?! The puffiness in my body, because of swelling due to inflammation from the *lack of recovery and rest time from exercise,* subsided. My body was healing itself by allowing it adequate rest. Below the surface of this, by allowing my body to rest, I was also letting go of my self worth being connected to what I produced. By making space in my day to rest I was stating " I am enough."

So part of my training protocol was identify when I was believing, feeling and thinking *I am not enough, I am not doing enough, I do not have enough—and therefore I cannot sleep, rest, until I am enough,* and inquire why? And was this true? I began to reframe the belief that I must be productive in this world to earn my worth. Of course, that was never going to happen because the ego would never let me experience "enough."

Enough is not quantifiable. So, I gave myself the permission to be enough, as I am, and permission to get some rest!

Nothing's Gonna Stop Me Now

In the 1980's, I saw the movie "Every Which Way but Loose" with Clint Eastwood. I vaguely remember the story line of the movie. What I do remember is watching Clint's' character go for a run while wearing blue jeans. When I saw this movie, it was during one of my "fat" years and at that time there were very limited options in sports clothing for larger women.

This was about the time the Jog Bra™ came out. After buying one, then testing it out, I discovered it didn't offer enough support for me. Brilliantly though, I just wore a regular bra underneath it. The combo then offered enough support for me to run comfortably. However, there were neither running pants nor shorts that would fit me. Not to be denied, after seeing Clint's character run with long jeans, that gave me the idea and permission to run in my jean cut-offs. So I did.

It was great. It felt like I was doing something for me, something I enjoyed doing. And the lack of specific sport clothing was not an excuse not to do it. I had figured out a way.

For a moment, I felt unstoppable.

Running offered me some freedom to use my mind and my body, instead of my mind using me. The time running was to sort things out, roll things around, look at my stuff from a different perspective—and, most of all, to ask questions about my own beliefs.

On some of these runs, in my jean cutoffs and double bra, I was occasionally taunted by people driving past. Angry people shouting or honking insults toward what their ego-filled minds thought of as *a fat girl running*. I *was* a fat girl running, yet I didn't care then because I was doing something, taking action, taking control of my own destiny through running. Most of the time, I didn't care what insults they yelled. I stayed with it. There were times, though, that I did feel small as they insulted me—hurt and emotionally vulnerable, out there on the road running, exposed.

Yet the running made me strong over time, both emotionally and physically. On one hand, I was running to lose weight, so I could eat what I wanted but not gain weight. On the other hand, I ran to know me—to empower myself, to flex my mental and physical muscles. It was part of my seeking to remember that *I was in there somewhere*, under all these layers. But not layers of flesh, layers of protection.

As I ran and juggled my weight and food intake like a check book—calories in and calories out to keep a balance—I occasionally found myself bingeing. The critical entity inside my head was back. Judging, criticizing, if only for a little while. Just long enough to cause some damage. I was still more focused on the outer form of me than the inner me, or at least more aware of my outer focus than the inner.

Once damaged by the binge, the only thing, the only tool I had at that time was to run to patch me up again. I was driven to run it off—the food, the calories, the guilt — after the binge. It was like being overdrawn on calorie expenditures—then *having to run to create a deficit*. This process made me feel so sick, to run on a full stomach, but again, I was driven to not gain the weight. As sick and yucky as I felt, I continued with this for several years.

The binge was about giving up on myself, my life, of ever wanting more out of my life. The running was about restoring hope. Not giving up. I didn't know this then. I thought the binge was about fighting against food, my appetite. But a deeper hunger was there that had nothing to do with food. My appetite for living.

Eventually I stopped running after a binge. It just wasn't worth it to feel so sick. I decided I would just live with the decision I had made in the moment: to over-eat, *then start anew the next day*. It was a step toward caring for myself. I chose not to run as a way to accept my behavior, for my overindulgence, and then let myself soften into it. I was slowly learning from the feeling, then altering the behavior. I was moving in the direction of love and compassion for myself.

What I want to share with all of you is this: No one has to wait to feel good. We can begin to feel good now. We can feel good about ourselves at any weight. We can follow through, and therefore build our confidence, by doing the things we say we will do with the intention to feel good. We can move our bodies with the intention of enjoying moving them— to be one with the body— and not with the intention to move because the goal is to lose weight.

Make up your mind to get healthy and feel good now. Then, like I did, don't let anything stop you!

Injury: Heed the Messenger

I have worked with many people who think the body is the *enemy*. At one point, I thought my body was, too. It's not. Injury, aches, illness, falling, etc. are signs from the body that things are off balance. The body is attempting to get your attention. The only way it knows how is by sending you physical signs. I love Louise Hay's affirmation which I still use to this day: "I listen with Love to the messages from my body."

If you don't listen to—or you are not aware of— the initial little niggles from the body, they will only get bigger and louder! So, I suggest you listen up! Listen, go slowly, keep listening to the body by feeling it. The body is the messenger. Don't shoot the messenger by overriding or ignoring its messages by not being present in it.

I recently asked an athlete I know to do this activity. She had been injured for a few months, but had a big race looming, so she hobbled on with her workouts. Not doing the race meant *failure* to her, which was not an option. When I asked her what her body would say if she didn't do the race, her quick response was, *"Relieved."*

Our bodies are so intelligent. The mind is there to process what the body is saying. Give your body more credit by listening to its guidance!

Bring Joy Into Your Sport

Instead of expecting your physical activity to entertain you or make you happy, experiment with bringing your true joyful nature *into* whatever activity you are doing. Instead of expecting running to give you joy, for example, bring your joy into the running—by expressing appreciation, gratitude, and creating awareness.

We expect things or activities to make us happy. Therefore when the thing or activity has been experienced or has ended, so isn't the happiness that it brought us. We are saying we are only happy with that thing or activity. That our happiness is in that. This leads us to look for the next thing or activity to make us happy. We are *constantly seeking* when we expect *things* or *activities* to make us happy.

I did this for many years. We are taught, though not consciously, to look outside of ourselves, to expect things or activities to bring us joy. The external, never-ending quest to look outside myself for the thing or experience that would declare I was "enough."

I was looking outside myself by using sport to bring me happiness. Sport was where I was looking for my self worth, and my performance outcome was my identity. The joy didn't really last, the training wasn't sustainable, and the race results where out of my hands. I would never stop moving, I just couldn't stop. How could I if the sport and the racing was who I thought I was? I kept looking for races, the next event, to give me that high. I was thinking I had to keep doing the racing so I could stay happy, to know myself. It was in that way a drug, helping me to keep active, to keep moving. It was a form of *numbing myself* from myself. The underlying truth was I did not feel I was enough *as I was*. This, sport, training, and racing was a good place to hide. Rest, though much needed, wasn't an option.

Of course, I could be joyful when not being active, but I had simply convinced myself otherwise. When I wasn't experiencing joy from the sport as the years rolled on, I even considered quitting. I had forgotten that joy is available to me at anytime. It is always a matter of perspective. I had forgotten to be grateful and appreciative.

It was not until 10 years into training, racing, and being competitive that I began to appreciate this time I have had to move my body. I became grateful for what my body could do. I began to notice the sensations in my muscles as I moved. The sensation of my muscles moving I termed *peak sensation* to remove any judgment.

I became more conscious of feeling my lungs expand with each breath and to be joyful I have breath!

Once again, I was appreciative of nature. I found great pleasure when I stopped expecting exercise to make me happy. I had been either unhappy or in search of the next sport or thing to make me happy. What a relief when I figured this out! I was free to express myself more openly and freely in all aspects of my life and could move on from exercise and still

be joyful. I no longer needed exercise, racing or training *to be or to define* my identity or to *feel* my joy.

I ask you to do the same. Don't relate your happiness, your joy, with your doing. Bring joy and happiness into your doing and not the other way around. If you don't practice this approach, then you will be looking for the next "high" in the form of a trip, race, or event to create the happiness. If you live this way, you are then always in a state of searching.

Being and Doing

What a relief to learn this. Being is not the same as doing, and who I am is not based on what I do. I had thought that people were more valuable based on what they did (and less valuable based on what they didn't do). Same for *who they knew* or didn't know. This is what is meant by God creating all men equally, equal in spirit and ability to create our own life experiences.

I used to think I was less important and less valuable for some specific reasons. Similarly, I have worked with women who do not exercise or do physical activities because they have been told from a very early age that they are not athletes or they are not coordinated to do sports. Instead, they have been told they are the "smart one," not the "athletic one," or told that girls just don't do sports. This became part of their story, and they made it part of their identity of who they believe themselves to be without ever challenging the validity of it. Who cares if you are "good" at sports or not? Well, they did!

These women were confusing who they are with what they did. Who you are is not determined by what you do. Who you are is energy, spirit, soul. And even these words don't explain, words can never take us that far, the words are mere pointers toward something undefinable. What we do is just that, what we do. Saying I an athlete creates a story, a mental construct of who I believe myself to be. I am energy, spirit, soul: that's the closest I can get using words. "Athlete" is referring to what I do. Be aware if you are over identifying yourself with what you do. Stay attune to the difference of who you are, being, and what you do, the doing. Be aware if you are playing a role and taking that to be who you are. Playing a role limits you in your life.

It wasn't until I could separate who I am from what I do that I had the freedom to *create and experience life differently*. When I saw myself as an athlete, I began to play the "role" of athlete. Doing this did not leave me much freedom or flexibility in creating other experiences that might not be in harmony with my role definition of "athlete." If I held my identity tightly of of who I am in being a triathlete, then who would I be when I stopped doing triathlons?

Such was the case when my inspiration to continue as a triathlete waned. I was *so over-identified as a triathlete*, I feared I would lose my sense of self, and self-worth if I stopped. So I stayed with it. It wasn't until I could separate doing from identity that I was able to also detach from the outcome of my competitions.

Each one of us has a story we latch on to and carry with us from childhood or from some event in our life. This story influences us greatly, and unless we are aware of this story, and who we really are, it can become habitual, creating and often unconsciously affecting the way our life is lived out.

It's best not to confuse function, doing, with identity. Change the story, let go of this old tale. Recognize and let go of your structure, it's not serving you. Break down old roles and beliefs. After all, all structures are impermanent. Challenge your old stories. You are not your sport, you are not your body. You are much bigger than any of that.

Failure

Opportunity for growth and learning come from failure. Failure is okay. It helps us clarify what works and what doesn't work, what we may want and what we don't want. Again, have comfort in knowing you can never *be* a failure. You can only do something that does not work out. I am here reminding you that we love one another as human beings, not human doings. What we do may not always be perfect, but on a deeper level, we already *are perfect*.

There's no need to identify yourself as a failure. Failure is attempting something new and different that did not work out, this time. *It* failed not you failed. Go back and do it again. Each time you fail, learn and grow from it. Allow yourself to be vulnerable in your attempt to do something different. Embracing failure can lead to personal growth, compassion and creativity. Feel the fear around failing; then do it anyhow!! Failure is only a problem if you think it so.

Take a moment, ask yourself what does failure mean to you? Bring this question into your writing, inquire about it, be curious and write. What would your life look like if you if you embraced failure? What does fear of failure keep you tied to?

We cannot have it both ways though. When something succeeds, it is something we did, not who we are. It was a success, not that we are success.

Mapping it Out

Start small and simple with your fitness plan and grow from there. As you bring awareness of what you are doing into your fitness activity, you may soon notice love and connection happen!

Consider your actual schedule. Do you really have space in your day to exercise every day? If you have not been doing any exercise thus far, I'd say start with *one day each week* to exercise. That's all. But commit to this one day. Set your ideal amount of time you can do this. If you can schedule 30 minutes one day each week, great. Start there. I then suggest you come up with a default time as well. Plan at least 10 minutes, if you can't get to the 30. When you do this, a few things will likely happen.

My experience with making changes, as I started to run, was to start with short walks or jogs, slowly, for 5-10-15 minutes. Each week I stretched the runs out a little more. I got to the point where I could run for 10 miles. Though as I was running and progressing and extending the length of my runs, I had a thought: *where does this stop?* I wondered if I would just keep going until I was running all day! Of course this would not be practical, and yet I was aware of this feeling of *it would never be enough.* Really, what I was saying was that *I* would never be enough.

I started slowly at first, 5 minutes running very slowly. I built it up over time. Eventually, I was running and competing in races. I started with three miles, then six miles, then 13 miles, and eventually up to marathons. My running developed slowly and progressively over a few seasons. As I ran, I learned about myself—my strengths and weaknesses. I thought about what I wanted for me, for my life. It was not always growth, fun, and progress. I was not only changing myself outside, but was changing myself inside. Somehow, through my persistence over 10 years, then 20 years, I came together. In discovering my body I was discovering my soul.

What I had noticed—as I began to make my own changes—is the negative entity that was in my head would try to talk me out of this activity. I went through this "mapping it out" exercise with a very busy working mom. On the first day of her activity—a 30-minute walk first thing in the morning—she woke too late to go for 30 minutes. She considered her 10 minute default plan, but then the negative voice piped in, "10 minutes. You'll never lose weight with just 10 minutes." She didn't go that day. This can be common, so deeply ingrained and habituated is the egoic voice. It can happen so quickly, you may not notice it at first.

Keep in mind that this isn't about losing weight. This is about creating a schedule to map out your plan to feel good. To get back in touch with your own *body intelligence* in a practical manner. I suggest you experiment with this. Set a simple goal—to be physically active 5 minutes every day, for example. Whatever it is, once you set your goal, follow through with it. By following through, you will build your confidence and trust in yourself—by keeping your word and promise to yourself, by not letting the voice in your head talk you out of it. Follow your first impulse to just get up and go before the negative voice wakes up!

It started small for me with my "no excuses" attitude as I ran in my double bra and cut-off shorts!

Be clear as to why you are being active: to be physically present in your body, enjoy nature, and use movement as an active meditation, for example. Let weight loss take care of itself as you focus on the real "food" of your life: connection, creativity, spirituality, movement, relationships, and career.

Next, your goal could be to keep your plan to incorporate exercise into your day and your week very simple. Pick a day or a few days in the week that you can exercise, based on your *pull*. Your pull is a sensation that comes from the body, an inspiration from within. Maybe it's to stand and stretch, bend over and touch your toes, or go out for a walk.

Consider what's available to you, where can you make room, realistically, in your schedule. What time can you afford, and what will be a step in the direction you want to go?

I heard a story of one very busy researcher who would set his alarm every 50 minutes. He would then take a 10-minute break to do calisthenics during that time. He'd then resume his work. Never underestimate the value of a few minutes here and there. It ads up in a day!

Be realistic in what you can do with your current schedule versus what you think you *should* do. One step at a time, not the whole staircase. If you can hardly create 10 minutes to yourself now, how will you create 30 minutes every day? That's risky at setting yourself up for more self-flogging if you cannot attain it. But then it could be an opportunity to practice "failing". Choosing 30 minutes doesn't work—it failed—you have learned that's not fitting your schedule right now. Not that you failed. Try something different.

Thirty minutes a day could be a long term goal, but for now, keep it simple and do- able. You will be creating new habits both mentally and physically.

You may experience the greatest success by following through and sticking with an exercise plan (and creating a new habit) because you mapped out what your plan will be for the week. Take 10-15 minutes each week to consider what will work, given your schedule. What class(es) might you want to attend? What days and times can you get out for a walk? Write it down, map it out.

When you do this, you set your thoughts and desires in motion. You are making a decision, and as

Ralph Waldo Emerson said, "Once you make a decision, the whole of the universe will conspire to make it happen." Keep your word and promises to yourself. Honor your personal time in your day. Stick with it; this is *your time*.

Knowing what to do to create a healthy body can be easy. It's the following through that can offer the challenge. Your new schedule—and break from old habits—will be subject to the *egoic thinking* in an attempt at self-preservation! You may wake up in the morning with the good intention of going for a walk, something new for you, only to be met with criticism from the voice in the head: "Don't go, don't bother. It's only a 10-minute walk. What good will that do? You will never lose weight with 10 minutes of walking"… and on it goes. It can talk you out of it. That voice can be so strong at first, but the more you come to realize it's there, the more transparency there is to it, *the more diminished* it becomes. Like white noise. A fan blowing in the distance.

Heart Rate

I started using a heart rate monitor when I started training for Triathlons—swimming, biking, and running. A heart rate monitor is a chest strap that goes against the skin to transmit the number of times the heart beats in a minute, which are then picked up by a receiver. Typically the receiver is a wrist watch.

These devices together offer bio-feedback on how easy or hard the heart is working. When I first got my monitor, I would wear it around the house during daily activities to observe how it would change. As I walked up the stairs, it, my heart rate, would go up; going down the stairs, I would see it drop back down. I was curious, and it was fascinating to see how my heart rate changed as my heart worked to get this body through a typical day.

As I started to use the heart monitor for training, I always tried to get my heart rate as high as possible, all the time—by pushing myself more, through more effort. Initially, I didn't allow myself rest days. It was always as much and as fast as possible.

This hard training served me for a little while. I did well in racing by improving my times and placing in my category. But over about eight years, with the constant hard effort, the limited resting, poor eating, my own mental stress, and the emotional roller coaster I was on—because of it all—my body started to crack.

Signs of it cracking were weight gain—even though I was exercising—dropping performance, fatigue, extreme mood shifts, and physical pain in my joints. The more weight I gained, the more I worked. The more I worked, the higher and longer my heart rate stayed elevated, the more weight I gained, the harder I worked. The harder I worked, the more I ate. I had created a crazy cycle.

I was eating lots of sugar too. I was eating lots of sugar because of the high heart rate—I was burning glycogen and glucose for fuel to sustain this intensity—which my body was craving because it then needed to replace what was used. I was also eating sugar daily for convenience plus I believed I would "burn it off." Eating sugar combined with the high heart rate meant the more my cortisol (fight or flight hormone) levels stayed elevated. And, this all caused this outcome in the process: *the more fat my body would store.* I was keeping myself in a constant state of stress, and my body was doing its best to manage it. Unfortunately, I was ignoring all the signs from my body. As a result, it continued to crack.

I let myself go down this path through the fall of 1998. That fall I was training for my first-ever Ironman Triathlon (1.2 mile swim, 112 mile bike followed by a 26.2 miles run). I was overtrained—training too much and not resting enough to allow my body to absorb all that I was doing—at which point I started back-sliding, gaining weight, and losing fitness. Yet I couldn't see this, and therefore I didn't stop it. Over identified was I with the ego.

One monumental moment that occurred, before the race, was on a day I was mountain biking with friends. I was falling off the bike on the roots and rocks while my friends cruised effortlessly along. At one point I was so mad, furious, frustrated and out of my mind, that I actually got off my bike and pushed it via rolling it down the trail *without me on it.* I stood trail side as I watched it bump, bounce and crash down the trail. From what I would now, upon reflection, call "insane moment," I then started to cry. My friends were in shock as they looked at me, wondering who had just stepped into my body! I couldn't recognize me either, whoever I was. I was a physical and

emotional wreck. So are the signs of being over trained, over stressed.

We think of exercising as being a positive stress, which it is. All things in moderation are good. A little stress helps us rise to our best self. A little exercise stress, along with rest, allows the body to adapt. And a little exercise can help to alleviate life stressors.

At this time, I had piled too much stress onto my system. I piled on the physical stress of exercising at high intensity, and high heart rate, but without sufficient resting and recovering. I had piled on the chemical stress in the form of eating too much (or rather eating only carbohydrates and sugar to fuel me). And, the added emotional stress of work I didn't enjoy—I didn't know about bringing my joy into what I do. I was using exercise as a means to both build my self-esteem or confidence *and beat myself up.*

As you can perhaps imagine, my first Ironman didn't go well in my mind. I did finish and it was a thrill. Yet—the "never enough, never good enough," negative egoic voice was not satisfied. Plus, I was still a physical and emotional mess.

I was about to quit racing triathlon; I had been at it for eight years at that point. I had pushed myself to the point of desperation. But as a result of this, I began to seek other ways of training. It wasn't me, it was my approach.

Eventually, as I learned how to use the heart rate monitor, I got the most out of it when I started doing *low heart rate training*.

I learned about and then adopted low heart rate training, and with that, I began to feel *renewed*. The low heart rate training involves keeping the heart rate low using a formula based on age. I used this formula of 180 (number of heart beats in one minute) minus my age = maximum aerobic heart rate. At the time I was 34, so I subtracted my age, 34, from 180. The 180 is assuming 180 is the highest your heart rate would be if you have a good aerobic system in place. For comparison, most people have a heart rate of 50 when they wake up in the morning. So 180 is more than three times what it is when resting.

I began to work at this heart rate of 145 (I rounded up) as a means to recover and heal my body. This meant I was riding my bike, running and swimming slower, much slower, than I had been. My muscles where strong, but my cardiovascular system was not very efficient.

This lower heart rate meant I was going slower than I was used to, but allowed me to tap into a different energy system. This meant I was utilizing more of my stored body fat to fuel my working muscles, rather than utilizing sugar (glucose, or glycogen) in my body. This burning more fat and less sugar meant I was less ravenous after a workout, and therefore less likely to find my hand in the cookie jar post exercise.

With low heart rate training, I was not depleting my stored sugar in my body, and therefore didn't need to *re-supply these stores* post exercise. Also, as I shifted my training to low heart rate, I began to get rid of the puffiness that resulted in consuming almost all carbohydrates and sugar in my diet. And I was less fatigued with a lower heart rate—which contributed to having more energy, less stress. I was resting more and the quality of my rest was significantly improved . The less sugar I ate, and the lower heart rate meant less stress on my hormonal system which then meant reduced inflammation in my body, so some joint pain I had been experiencing diminished and then went away. Most importantly I was improving my fitness, having a more enjoyable experience with the easier effort, and being kinder to my body. It all translated into a happy, healthier and more rounded *me*.

The reason I mention this is that it helped me to feel better about myself. If you want to exercise and feel good, then get a heart rate monitor. It can offer biofeedback if you are working at too high a heart rate or if you are working at to low a heart rate and would get more benefit by getting it higher. Once you have one you must use it to get the benefits which means you will need to get out there and move!

I see well-meaning individuals start up an exercise class then go at it for a few weeks. They work really hard and sweat a lot during it. This is great! I'm glad to see people up and moving. But I wonder if it would be more helpful and more sustainable if each person knew their own heart rate during their activity. The trend for example, especially around the New Year, is to join a club with the intention of exercising, getting in shape. People go to classes, workout for a few weeks and then slowly fall off. I wonder if, one, they didn't bite off an unrealistic goal of exercising five days a week, when before they were never going to the gym. Instead of five days, go for one day.

Once you are consistent with one day, add a second day. Once that has become a habit, add a third day. Gradually build, and be consistent. From zero days to one day is a step.

Second, I consider that if people did cardio work with the heart rate parameters of 180 minus their age equaling their max aerobic heart rate, I think they would enjoy it more and be more likely to continue.

My thinking is thus: working at this max aerobic heart rate may feel easier, and therefore more enjoyable, so with that experience it may be more likely that the person would continue. You would be burning a higher percentage of fat for fuel, and you'd be utilizing less sugar to fuel the body—and therefore be less likely to crave carbohydrates after. Using this max aerobic heart rate seems more sustainable and results in less stress in the body. It builds a more solid foundation for a strong cardio system. You may be burning less total calories, but you'll be training your body to be more efficient and better at managing stress.

It's extremely helpful to have this information to get the most out of your exercise or training time. The theory is when exercising at this maximum aerobic heart rate, you will likely be burning a larger percentage of body fat to fuel your working muscles. At this heart rate, you will be teaching your body to be *more efficient at burning fat*. Once you start to go above this number, you will likely begin to burn a larger percentage of stored sugar in the body to fuel the working muscles—as opposed to the fat burning.

This max aerobic heart rate can be more effective in training your aerobic system than working at a heart rate number above your max aerobic heart rate. The max aerobic heart rate tends to burn more fat and is teaching your body to be more efficient metabolically. What this means is your body will not have to work so hard to keep it running, literally!

As your body becomes more efficient through this type of heart rate training, you will notice over time that you can go faster than when you started the program, yet still be at this max aerobic heart rate. You will also have to push your effort a little more to keep your heart rate in your max aerobic zone, another sign of improvement. You thus have developed a solid aerobic base to build from. In essence, exercising becomes easier! You have become more fit.

You may be surprised at how slow you will need to go at first. You may be barley moving at this max aerobic heart rate. So walking, cycling, running, doing Zumba, using the Stairclimber, and so forth would all best be done in this heart rate range, or zone. For some of you, this could be very slow for you. That's okay; this is feedback that your aerobic system is in need of some slow time. Hang at this low heart rate for a month or two and see if your pace doesn't gradually change—or get faster over time as your aerobic system improves by becoming more efficient.

This works best when you stay very, very committed to this slow effort and do it over time. You will be utilizing more fat, less sugar for fuel as you improve on both your aerobic and fueling system.

The cost of a heart rate monitor can range from as low as $50 for a simple basic model to over $800 for one with lots of features. Having a simple watch that shows the time of day, your heart rate, and it has a stop watch feature with a lap counter, would be a sufficient entry-level step.

Passing Health Along

Where do we get our messages about our bodies from? My messages first came from my mother and other women around me. Then when I entered school, they came from teachers, other kids, and adults around me—plus messages from magazines, the news, television, etc. They also came from my response to situations as I interpreted them through my own eyes.

Mothers pass along their stories to their daughters. Daughters then carry the torch to pass along those stories they learned from their moms to their daughter(s). And so it goes. It continues along. *Unless the cycle can get broken.*

In a conversation I had with a young mom I was working with, who is currently not happy with her body, it reminded me how this happens. A part of me was still surprised this cycle still does happen. I was thinking because I had learned certain lessons, so did everyone else.

During a meeting, the mother expressed her concern that her young daughter may one day become embarrassed by her, by her weight as a large mom. The mom recognized she didn't want this experience for her daughter so she was being careful about conversations she had with people about her weight, or food issues, while her daughter was around. This was perhaps helpful, except that she was silently passing along the message in other ways. Though she was careful with her language, her non-verbal cues were still there.

Messages don't have to be passed along verbally, especially with kids. They are smart and can pick up on things. I saw a mom out walking briskly this morning in my neighborhood. A young teenage girl was walking with her. I assumed it would be her daughter. What crossed my mind was that I was hoping they were walking together to bond, to be outside, to be in nature, and to share in the joy of moving their own bodies, feeling their own physical strength. But I thought not.

Given my own experience, and hearing the experiences of other moms I know, the walking could likely be about exercising to lose weight or control weight or to burn up enough calories to think they now *deserve* to eat, or, to burn enough calories to then feel they can eat cake or dessert. Is the exercising about punishment for the food they over-indulged in, a form of punishment for their sin, the sin of eating? I would love to believe the exercising was about celebration, of exercising for the sake of exercising without looking for an outcome besides the pure enjoyment of it. To feel the aliveness within. I hope they are using this time to talk and to bond.

I know this is not the message that moms want to pass along—that exercising is a must, that exercising is about losing weight, or a punishment. I would like to see exercise as a form of love, not fear. A way to care for the body, connect to it and connect to the spirit. I'd like to ask everyone, competitors and non- competitors, to view exercise as a time to experience *mind, body and spirit in harmony*. There will not be harmony and love if it's done out of fear. Pass health along, mothers to daughters, through living, loving examples.

In the Name of Love! Part 1

It is my wish that all of you reading this book will exercise, or partake in some form of physical activity, as a gesture of *Love for the body*, your body, the body your spirit is housed in. I say this from my experience of many, many years of focus on physical activity or sport as a means to lose weight, control my weight, burn off calories from the food I just ate (or am about to eat) and/or as a means to beat my body, and therefore myself. I did this out of abuse, to get this body to conform into something it was not in that moment— or at least to conform to my perception of it.

Little did I realize then that my dissatisfaction with my body, my physical appearance, was a message coming from deep within. These messages came from a place I couldn't identify at the time, a place, a message I had no words for then. In a sense, through distrust of my body and abusing it through exercise I was shooting the messenger, this body, my body, the one housing my soul, my spirit. My spirit was talking to me through my body; I simply wasn't having any of it. I thought my body was the enemy at that time, from my level of consciousness or awareness. The only thing I knew to do, and was taught to do, was attempt to beat it into submission.

I see this in many women of all ages, shapes, and sizes today. It's encouraged in all media outlets. The underlying message: We are needing to get this out-of-control body under control. And if we do, we will be happy. We will be just the right size. And for any competitive female athletes, we will have a better performance.

I suggest a different approach. This is what I have done; this is why I have been successful with having lost 60 pounds and having kept it off. I have not kept the weight off because of exercise. I have kept the weight off because of all I do *to love this body I am in*, which is to say the life that I have sculpted. Exercising being one of my choices. It's because I do, or practice, my physical activity as an act of love for myself, for this body, for the body that houses my spirit, my soul. Never again do I want to eat some food that is "bad" for me, only to then feel compelled to go "run it off" to make me feel whole or in control again. For those of you who have done this or are still practicing this, you know what I mean. You know what this feels like. It does not feel good either emotionally or physically. Instead of using the running as a form of punishment for the food you have eaten, show love and kindness for yourself.

Accept the decision you have made around eating the food, sit with it. Take a deep breath. Bring yourself back into your body in the current situation, in this current moment. We all behave certain ways for perfectly good reasons. The food is doing something for you. Your work is to figure out what it does for you. In discovering the why, it will make sense to you and then you will be free to choose differently. You will be okay; you will live through this moment. Show kindness and acceptance, over and over toward yourself. You are not diminished in any way by the "doing". You are still the same beautiful being. See through to that.

FOOD

"Eating well is a critically important life skill."
Michael Pollan

The Choices We Make

Our most basic reason to eat is to stay alive, by providing building material for the body to operate, and to fuel it to move about. But we also eat for taste, social reasons, and cultural expression—to name a few. *Why* we eat what we do can also be about fear, habit, cost, availability, education, the list is endless.

But there was one reason I was eating more than what my body needed to stay operational. Eating more than what I needed, thus overriding messages from my body, whether it be full or hungry, was like not going to the bathroom when I needed to—or going to the bathroom when I didn't need to.

During my earlier years, food was a survival mechanism. I used it to numb myself. I was not making *conscious choices* when I was eating. Of course at first, I was eating what my parents were offering.

Once I hit middle school though, which is when I started to dislike school *as well as dislike my body*, I started to care more about what I was eating. Which means I was eating anything and everything. This is when I started to eat as a means to escape from middle school years and all the emotions that come with that period of time. I used food to numb myself to avoid intimacy, to avoid pain, to stuff down feelings I was taught were wrong—feelings of inadequacy, fear, insecurity, and more. Whenever I was stressed, I reacted to it by eating. Though I choose food to numb—instead of alcohol, work, or drugs—it was my "drug" of choice to numb myself from the challenges of life and my perception of them. I used it as my life preserver.

I see well-meaning dietitians, fitness professionals, wellness workers, etc. working with people to help them lose weight. They believe that if the person they are working with, trying to help, *knew to eat the right food,* and then chose to eat those foods, then they would lose weight and be healthy. They don't ask them, "What do you want the food to do for you?, or what does eating when you are not hungry do for you?"

We look at most of these people and see how their excess weight is hurting them, but no one thinks to ask how the extra weight is *helping* or serving them. Their fat or excess weight must be providing some sort of benefit for them. Otherwise, they would have shed the extra pounds that seem to be making their lives miserable to begin with.

Weight is not a tragedy unless we make it so. We see it as a "bad" thing. But, by seeing through all the pain and suffering it seems to create for each individual, the awakening can lift us to a higher and deeper joy, a mindset of gratitude and appreciation.

For me, it was an awakening to being *the creator of my own life experience*. My weight had little to do with what foods I chose to eat. I couldn't, or wouldn't, let go of the pain and suffering until I could discover all of the blessings of my awakening. With it came a new form of simplicity. No amount of fruits and vegetables was going to do that for me.

What's good for us?

Ask almost anyone what they could do to change or improve their diet and they will say "eat more fruits and vegetables." This is great, simple, so why don't they then follow through and eat more fruits and vegetables—if they know this would improve their health and how they feel?

What's good for us varies and changes with time. It's fluid, like all of life is. No single diet fits all—

although I encourage foods "closest to the dirt," meaning less processed and mostly plants.

Most of us know what to eat, that is to say what is healthy for us, but not many of us are actually choosing those foods that most nourish us. Individuals may be aware that what they are eating is not the best for the body, yet *they are not taking the steps to change it once this is recognized*. They are stuck where they are, but not knowing the reason. During one of my workshops, one participant told me about her desire to eat food that is in her words "terribly, horribly bad for you." My question is why would you want to eat anything your term "terribly, horribly, bad for you?" What are you saying about the value of your life if this is what you are choosing?

I have heard people say their body is craving something, or they just couldn't stop eating even though they felt full. As though the body just couldn't stop. So often we separate the body from the mind, as though the body is the enemy acting individually, on its own, creating the problem. I feel it's the opposite. It's the egoic mind that acts as the devil on the shoulder, provides temptation or the thoughts that cause us to self-sabotage. Or, it's the thoughts that over-ride what the body is experiencing—fullness. Use the mind to sense what you are *feeling* in the body and then use words to be able to describe what you feel. Go to the body to sense, use the mind to interpret.

It seems so easy to say you will do something healthier, take steps, change. But then, the challenge is to be transparent and on guard to the voice of temptation—the one that says "give up, it won't work, it never does, why bother?" It's not the food, it's not the body, it's that *little voice in the head* that keeps one stuck, that carries and perpetuates the stories. Deconstruct the stories.

Some people don't know what is healthy to eat. There are so many mixed messages in the media that lead to confusion. We no longer trust ourselves. Sometimes I wonder if there is a conspiracy and that "someone" wants us all to be confused so "they" can sell us something. One week the message is to eat this food, the next week that food is suddenly unhealthy. There are ads everywhere for the next miracle food or diet, which is forever changing. There are the people who need education around food. Once they learn more about healthier choices, and make the changes, they become healthier. Theirs is the case of needing education.

Then there are people who eat what they do because of what is available or not available to them. They may or may not have the financial resources to pay for the healthier stuff. Or they don't have access to healthy food due to proximity of grocery stores or transportation to one. Theirs is the case of limited availability. If they get help with money or transportation they can improve their health.

Then there are people who say they want to be healthier by eating nutritious food, lose weight, and get in shape (this was me). They start off with the best intentions but then hit a wall or stop all together. Hmmm. This is where I ask how keeping the weight on, or not sticking with making changes, is serving you?

One reason not to change is because staying where we are serves some kind of purpose. The fun is in figuring out what that purpose is.

And the second reason not to change is because reaching for food is a habitual response deeply ingrained. Ego response. You have to break the habit physically of reaching for food and the habitual unconscious desire to reach for food (the habitual ego response) that leads to the *reaction*—to eat—versus action. Which takes awareness.

Why Bother

I remember a time in high school where I decided I was going to lose weight, get in shape, and feel good about myself. I would get up early in the morning, packed all my clothes for the day, and then I walked a mile to the YMCA pool alone. I swam with what seemed like a gazillion adults all swimming before work.

I recall feeling I was going to drown with all the turbulence from so many swimmers in the pool! After swimming, I showered, changed and walked to high school. I don't recall if I brought food or money to buy food from the cafeteria or not. I do recall feeling good for having done the swim. I don't recall how long I kept this up. But I do recall one afternoon when back at home, while I was eating something, one of my parents flipped out and said to me: "Why do you bother exercising? You just eat twice as much!" Ouch, crushed! "They are right," chimed the ranting in voice my head.

My parents never had the words to actually express what they really wanted to express. They approached life from a place of fear, and this was no different. What I would later come to learn, as they told me, is they feared that if I was "heavy," or "solid," as they often used to say, *that no one would love me*. In that moment of their fearful words, I thought so, too. Who would love me if I was fat? Who would love me if I didn't love myself either? If my parents saw me as fat, did this mean they didn't love me? Who would love me then, if my parents didn't love me? Is size of the body an indicator of how lovable someone is? I didn't swim again.

In hindsight, it would have been great had I been strong enough to have not paid any attention to my parents fears—and to acknowledge that I was doing this in part *to feel good and not just as an activity to lose weight*. I can simply use this story as a pointer back then to what I did want: to feel good.

There is so much wrapped in this story, though I would not change a thing about it, as it has taught me so much about me, my resiliency, and my passions to name a few.

I'll Skip the "Syrup"—a true turning point

After an evening binge, I think it was during my high school years, I took some Ipecac syrup. Ipecac syrup is meant to be taken in an emergency situation if someone has swallowed poison. It is meant to induce vomiting to rid the body of the poison.

Taking the Ipecac post binge was a premeditated act, as I had it on hand for this moment. I believe I had read about this syrup stuff or maybe heard about it around school. I knew about sticking your finger down your throat to make yourself vomit which I attempted once, but could never actually commit to it long enough in the moment to actually empty my stomach, which was the point.

I don't recall the steps to me buying the Ipecac syrup, or even where or how I hid it from my family, but I had it. I thought it would be salvation in a glass bottle to being able to eat whatever I wanted and not gain weight. To have a different life because anything would be better than the life I had now. Now post binge, I went to my rescuer, followed the directions, and waited. It didn't take long.

Prior to this behavior, I will say that I never liked to feel sick. I am the one that when sick, I'm making deals with God: *Please God, let me feel better now and I will never take my health, my feeling good for granted ever again!*

So here I was so desperate, and so connected to my egoic thinking, that I was taking something that *made me sick!* It was terrible. An awful feeling to have something inside of me—only to realize I had made a mistake as my stomach started to fold, my mouth water. *Vomiting is such a violent act* in my opinion. *What the fuck have I done?* is what I thought as I lay over the toilet seat. It was no longer just about the food I had binged on that I wanted out of my system. There was no "undo" button, but if there was, I would have used it. *I had sunk to an all-time new low.* I had double regret, and double the reason to condemn myself—one, for the binge and two, for being so stupid to take this stuff, to make myself sick. How outta control could I be?

I got my wish, it *all* came out.

At one point, as I lay flopped over the toilet seat— that in itself is humiliating—my brother knocked on the door to check on me, likely from hearing me hurling. I remember he seemed suspicious of the whole scene. But I lied to him, and thus had lied to myself.

This is not a proud moment for me. But I share it as it acts as a pointer as to the depth of my despair— the depth of my inability to see the real truth, and my attempt on my part to get rid of what I thought the problem was: *How to stop being fat.*

Though I did empty my gut, and therefore all the *extra calories* from the binge (which was the ultimate goal of the whole event—success in that part) I never did the Ipecac again. I did however binge again, though this moment was a pivotal point for me. I was *pivoting from* my outward desperation. I knew at least I was not willing to go that route to *recover* from a binge-vomiting in order to solve my fat problems.

So deep into my own self-destruction then, at that moment. How did I find my way out? Again I couldn't, or wasn't going to let it, the weight, the fat, the sabotage, go until I discovered its blessings.

How We Eat

Do you make eating a sacred or near-sacred event? Feeding your body that houses your soul? Or, do you eat like you're on your way to a fire?—as though this will be your final meal (this was me), taking everything you can because you never know if there will be more? Do you eat with great attention?

Whatever you notice yourself doing, see if you can create a scene of calm, as you eat relaxed, tasting your food, sitting down at a table, savoring each bite, no stress and no distractions (computer, talking on the phone, television, etc).

My eating was often not relaxed. It was rushed and simultaneously filled with pleasure, guilt, and shame at the same time. I wanted to slow down. I wanted to enjoy it and feel civilized about eating.

If you are not relaxed at each meal, start small, as I did. Add in one meal within your week where you can schedule in time for you to sit down and dine. Become aware of at least one bite. Make the eating your entertainment, so no TV, iPad, laptop, email, videos, etc. to distract you. Dial into the experience of eating. Skip the multitasking. What can you notice? Is there anything new about this experience—even though you have eaten every day all the days of your life—is there something new and different in this experience of eating *with intention*? With silence?$

When we are aware of our eating, we are present to our life. Yes, we have better digestion and we absorb the nutrients of the food better, too. Those are more physiological bonuses, which are important for our health and function of the body. But also, when tuned to our eating, we are expressing a love for the self. This can have much deeper meaning in our life than the nutrients of the food, or how well they get absorbed into the body. Conscious eating becomes a sign of love and reverence for the self—a symbol of gratitude for the body, for time here on this Earth, by being present to it happening! It's an action that says: *I see me, I exist and I matter.*

Take a deep breath, settle in, allowing joy into your dining experience. Eat with pleasure and purpose.

Athlete Eating

As an athlete, it's important to recognize the signs of hunger. Exercising can mask the typical hunger pangs, felt in the stomach that most of us are familiar with, because it suppresses the appetite. With the exercising masking the need to eat, especially right after a workout, hunger can seem to suddenly descend— leaving us ravenous as the effects of the exercise wear off.

Feeling desperately hungry post exercise can leave us grabbing for the nearest source of food, regardless of the quality of it. Quality food is important for all of us since what we eat becomes our body. The saying "you are what you eat" is literally true.

Being aware of post exercise nutrition is key to refueling with quality food that is going to help the body recover (by letting it heal from the workout and allowing it to rebuild stronger with the food consumed). With good post exercise nutrition you can come back stronger, have increased energy and improved fitness.

This can be challenging if you have a disorder or challenges around eating, as I did. My tendency was to sabotage the effort I had just put in by not refueling post exercise, which should have provided the recovery building material to bring me back better and stronger.

We want to heed the messages from the body, including hunger. Hunger is internal feedback letting us know when the body needs more food for fuel to keep it running, or rebuild it post exercise. And yet, overriding these messages, by either eating or not eating when you are not experiencing hunger signals, or eating beyond fullness, can possibly lead to new challenges.

If we over identify ourself as "athlete," we become conditioned to think, *I am an athlete*, and therefore believe *I need to, have to, or should be eating more.* The initial thought is that post exercise: *I need to eat to start to recover.* However, we may then forget or ignore the signs and signals of real hunger from the body, to *feel* hunger, as we condition ourselves to eat in a particular way, because we wear the hat of "athlete."

On the other hand, being an athlete seems to justify, at least in the mind of the ego, that we can eat whatever we want whenever we want. The reason for this response being, we believe, that as an athlete we need more fuel. It seems to become more of a *role*, athlete, we are playing than something we do, sports. We then start to eat out of habit or even because it's part of *our role as athlete*, and not out of need. "Athlete" becomes more of a mental construct. Instead tuning in to the needs if the body, we tune into the role constructed in the mind, or developed from habit.

To problem-solve this you start by increasing your awareness of when you are eating out of habit, or you are playing the role of athlete, rather than eating because of hunger. It can be tricky to separate them at first, but you may need to be asking yourself *is this hunger, habit, or a role I am playing?* Is your eating a reaction to having just exercised? Or are you truly hungry?

On the other hand—this is where it can get tricky if you have been emotionally/compulsively eating—you want to learn to eat out of need, as opposed to out of habit, to not deny the needs of the body. This could be a fine line which is why awareness, being tuned in to the ebb and flow of the body, is important. With consciousness, you will *know* the difference.

Signs that the body needs fuel (besides hunger pangs) that I have personally experienced are: irritability, low energy, mood swings, impulsiveness, indecisiveness, foggy thinking, lack of inspiration, poor performance, and lack of improvement. Becoming aware of these helped me identify for myself when I would truly need to eat, when I had taken not eating too far, to long, and how to use food to care for my body.

I have also learned that not eating enough calories, whether I'm exercising or not, causes the body to slow its metabolism down. Thus, if you are not eating adequate calories, the body will do two things—depending on how far and how long you take this practice of under-eating. One, it will break down by starting to use muscle tissue to fuel the body. So instead of getting stronger, you will grow weaker over time.

Second, the metabolism will slow down to adjust the body's need for calories—as it starts to conserve the calories it is taking in for the function of the body (digestion, breathing, pumping blood, etc.) Eventually, limiting calories will have the opposite of what you desire. You'll have less energy, more irritability, a decline in fitness, and weight gain.

As a recovering compulsive/emotional eater and athlete, I came to realize that awareness of these issues helped me understand real hunger from impulsive/stress related eating and separate the two. My thinking around this had been skewed because of my previous experience as an emotional eater. I needed to know, to learn, how and when to feed my athletic self and when I might be feeding my "negative" emotions by eating, or overeating.

I want to note here how important it is to not label ourselves as emotional/compulsive eaters. That would be another role identity. It is something we have done, but not who we are.

My experience has been that by *not recovering sufficiently*, over time, I found myself completely backsliding by losing fitness. This was because of improper food choices or insufficient food to rebuild those working muscles. I just wasn't growing stronger because I was not providing the food to make that happen.

By not providing enough of the good food, too much sugar, too many meals or snacks of carbohydrates only, and too many simple carbohydrates (white flour, sugar, pasta for example), foods that are high in calories but not nutrient rich, I found myself gaining weight despite all the exercise I was doing. It took a while to realize this and then allow myself to eat better food and to allow myself to rest. It took time to accept that if I put junk food into this exercising body, then I was going to get *junky inconsistent performance* back. I just wasn't providing the rest needed and the rebuilding blocks for this body to grow strong after each workout. I realized I was self-sabotaging, caught in a simple sugar vortex.

Many athletes are getting savvy to healthy eating to fuel their sport. I had to learn this. I started with a "calories in" and "calories out" mindset, which in the long term, didn't work for me

I ate cookies for breakfast when training for my first Ironman. One of my training days was: bike two hours, stay at friends, then bike back in the morning. Cookies in the evening, usually pizza too, then more cookies for breakfast the next morning. I was stressing my body with too much sugar and not enough nutrients. To the body, stress is stress whether it be physical, emotional, or chemical (food is considered a chemical stress). This led to my body   really "cracking"—breaking down given the signs of weight gain, mood swings, mild injuries which lead to my ever decreasing performance. But most importantly lead to me not feeling healthy, fit, nor strong. My body was set up for the fight or flight scenario where my cortisol levels stayed high so the fat burning signal was not turned on, but the "store the fat" signal was. These we're natural consequences of not paying attention to my body. Everything in my body said stop and rest.

Instead I listened to the mind; "more, faster, and harder!"

It did matter what I was eating, clearly, as my body was trying to tell me: *We are going over the edge! Move over, sugar and processed stuff. Bring on the real food!*

Real Food

Food has really changed since I was a kid. I remember having more real food available to me as a kid *that tasted like food.* There was less processed food back then. Or, if the food was processed, it seems it was less so than it is today. We had our share of chips and baloney, but we had fresh bread from a bakery and veggies from our garden. In the winter we didn't have mangos, tomatoes, or strawberries, summer seasonal fruit that is available to us now all year round.

On the surface, it seems nice to have these seasonal foods offered year round, but in winter months, I don't think they taste like anything! They are devoid of taste. No wonder kids don't like veggies or stay away from the grainy apples! Yuk.

There are so many food options out there today. The grocery stores are chocked full of stuff. I can't say that they are full of food. I'd say they are full of lots of *food-like substances.* Many highly processed, packaged foods, as well as fruits and vegetables that have traveled far and have likely been grown in nutrient-depleted soil. What we see in the store is grown and produced to look good so we buy it, but unfortunately it's not grown for taste.

I have noticed there are advertisements out there creating an image that obtaining and preparing real wholesome food is hard, time-consuming and costly. We are not being marketed the fresh whole carrots, for example, but carrots that have been washed and peeled for us. And they are coated, so they stay fresher and more appealing to the eye longer.

When shopping, go for the real stuff! That is to shop the perimeter. Go for the whole fresh foods as much as possible. These items are typically on the perimeter of the store. The fruits and veggies, dairy, eggs, meats, potatoes, butter, yogurt. Down the aisle you will look for nuts and seeds, breads, grains (oats, rice, flour).

I suggest you avoid the prepackaged, processed food-like substances. I know these packaged foods may be convenient, but they should not be the foundation of your eating. You must make time in your schedule each week to plan your meals, as well as *pre*-prepare your meals. This may mean devoting some time on the weekend to cook, slice, and dice food for the week—so you can create healthy meals when you want, especially when you're tired and hungry (which is when it can be easier to reach for the stuff that's not-so-good for you). The not-so-good for us stuff may be convenient and feel good going down, but not so good an hour or two later.

Just because you are an athlete does not mean you get a free pass to eat whatever you want. It's *not* calories in and calories out. Well it can be calories in and calories out, but you may then experience the natural consequences such as poor performance, illness, and low energy to name a few. Think wholesome food for a wholesome being.

Tired Eating

I noticed that I tend to eat more when I am tired. This makes perfect sense, since signs of tiredness are the same as signs of low blood sugar. These signs are yawning, feeling like you are in a fog, daydreaming, poor memory, sluggishness, feeling spacey, having lack of energy. When blood sugar is low, these are the types of symptoms related to it. The body is sending signals that it needs some energy. You then act on this by eating to provide the energy or fuel the body is asking for. Simple.

Again, when the body is tired, the same signals appear. How does one determine if it's fatigue or hunger? If after eating, things don't turn around for you—as in energy doesn't return or the mental fog doesn't dissipate—then it may be safe to say *the body is tired*. The remedy for a tired body would be sleep. Going to bed early, or leaving time to sleep in the morning, is the ticket, not more food.

Unfortunately, in our fast-paced always "doing" society, most will find the nearest cafe for a giant dousing of coffee to get them going in the morning, keep 'em cranking through the afternoon, then more coffee in the evening to finish up the day. Or, it's grab some sugar or any food that's quick and easy to give the body a boost. This only masks the problem, because what's needed is sleep, not more calories or more caffeine. In the case with food, it's easy to overeat as the body keeps looking for a way to solve its tiredness. But the body or mind is never satisfied because low blood sugar is not the problem, so food is not the solution. Sleep is the solution for a tired body, not excess food. The excess food is contributing to an unhealthy body. It's actually robbing the body of energy, not creating more!

I Eat What My Body Wants

Nowadays I have *no rules* around eating nor the foods I can or cannot eat. Who is to say what is healthy for me, is me. My body. I do eat chocolate, desserts, donuts and sugar, sometimes. *I have created awareness of when I have had too much of them based on how my body feels,* not the "food rules" floating around out there.

I had to *know* this on my own. I had to play with this, to let go of structures—let go of food rules—those self imposed, from society, food science, dietitians, diets, etc. I had to *feel* what my body needed not what my head—my mind—wanted. My mind was confusing because it held the stories, the structures. But it's my body, our bodies, that hold the wisdom, the truth of how we feel when I eat.

I started by eating whatever my body wanted, when I wanted it. I stopped when I had enough, when I was satisfied. I stopped or let go of thinking, the guilt I carried about eating, especially about certain foods deemed "bad." I ate the stuff I was told was "bad" for me such as cookies, and ice cream. I had to do this to let go and challenge the structures around what foods I should and should not eat. I had to experiment and find out for myself. To trust my body again.

It was scary for me at first to eat whatever I wanted to let go of guilt and habitual beliefs. But eventually two things notable happened, I felt less stressed and focused on food, and I started to actually crave real wholesome food.

About a week into eating whatever I wanted, a tractor trailer truck passed me on the road that had a picture of cornucopia of food displayed on the side. When I saw that image of food my mouth watered, it looked so good to see fruits and vegetables, meat, and eggs. I craved real food after eating so many dessert foods. It was most noticeable that my body actually wanted the "good" stuff because it did. Not because that's what I am supposed to eat or that's what's good for me. I had opened a new door.

There doesn't have to be rules or restrictions around eating when you trust yourself through awareness, you can trust your body.

For example, if I have had a few days of eating sugary foods, I begin to notice that just *thinking* of eating more sugar doesn't seem very appealing. In fact my teeth ache thinking about it! Just imagining consuming sugar or something sweet is not inviting. I recognize this as my body in its infinite wisdom is self regulating by saying—that's enough for now. But we must have awareness of the body to notice these messages as well as having let go of the guilt around such foods. We must be paying attention to and having a connection between body and mind to hear the message then heed it.

I remember one food "rule" I attempted to live by, but of course it didn't work, but here's what I realized.

My "rule" was to only allow myself to eat dessert on Saturdays. This meant of course no dessert all week long until I got to Saturday. On Saturday I could eat any dessert I wanted. But often when Saturday came I didn't really want to eat dessert. I did eat it anyhow, because it was Saturday and that was my rule.

I ignored my body and followed my rule and ate dessert. Then a very sad feeling washed over me post dessert. The high, like a drug, the longing, the anticipation I felt from the dessert, the special treat, was now gone. The high was short lived. It would be a very long slog until next Saturday when I could get another dessert "fix" again. It felt like such a let down. Dessert would never satisfy because that's not what my longing was about. Also, had the highlight of my life become about dessert on Saturday?

And what about if my body wanted dessert on Wednesday? I couldn't eat dessert then because it was Wednesday, not Saturday. Dessert rule is Saturday, not Wednesday. Yet, in an attempt to avoid dessert on the other 6 days of the week, I found myself eating twice as much as I tried to "dance around" eating dessert.

It clearly didn't work. I still ate when I wasn't hungry, I was still overeating, and I was still not heeding the messages from my own body. So I dropped the food rules, I felt in the long run, it wasn't working.

This took awhile, to eat whatever my body wanted, to let go of rules, structure. I had to keep coming back to it to figure it out for me. Also, my meals are not gourmet, usually foods I have on hand that I put together-no recipes, no fuss, mostly vegetables. Once in awhile I try a new recipe, but mostly I keep my meals simple. I eat what tastes good, feels good and what feels healthy because I want to out of love. And of course there is room for a little sweetness, too!

A Tip On Eating

Sit and relax and enjoy the food you are eating. Treat yourself like the goddess you are by taking time to consume foods that taste good, feel good in your body, and eat until satisfied. Make it an experience you remember. Eat to show love for who you are, for yourself. Consume wholesome, nourishing food that you want to eat because you want to eat it. You choose this food as a sign of love for who you are.

I have noticed, at times, when I was preparing food or when I was sitting to eat that my stomach felt a little upset, clenched. This was a sign for me that I was not relaxed. I might be anxious, feeling I should hurry to get the meal prepared or hurry up and eat because I had other more important things to do. I had so much on my to-do list, so much on my mind, that I felt I had to rush through my meal and get this eating out of the way to do that more important thing.

When I have realized myself rushing, or feeling anxious, which is the same as not being present—that is to say I became aware of my rushing, that I had anxiety in me—I would stop myself from what I was doing to then do something that was more relaxing. "Eating is important", I would remind myself. I didn't want to eat while experiencing anxiety or feeling rushed. I wanted to teach myself to eat while calm, present, so I interrupted the old habit by stopping the eating until the anxious thought and feeling had subsided. I have even gotten as far as plating my food to only then realize *I wasn't ready to eat*. At which point, I left my food and went to do something else, like sit on the couch to flip through a magazine or answer some emails—or sit outside to just relax by looking at the trees and listen to the birds. I did this because I realized if I ate in an anxious state I wouldn't enjoy the food I was eating, and it wouldn't bode well with my digestion of it. I figured I could do something else until I felt calm again.

A result of this break, this stopping, this interruption, I did enjoy the meal. I tasted and appreciated my meal by then being more present and relaxed in the process of eating. Through this, I would also be aware of when I was satisfied. Through this awareness, it typically kept me from over-eating as it allowed me to be in my body, in control to decide, to be aware—and not let the emotion carry me out of my body.

But, whether you are going to binge eat, compulsively eat, or eat nourishing food—whatever choose to eat—at least sit down to do it and pay attention.

Nourish An Active Body

Nourishment for an active body comes in two forms: one is food—to fuel, sustain, as well as rebuild muscles for the body—and two is to nourish the body *with quality rest.*

Rest is an often overlooked form of nourishment for the body, but without it, neither the activity nor the food will be properly absorbed into the body. The body needs the building blocks, in the form of food, to rebuild the muscles from a physical activity. And the rest is when this happens.

During activity, there are tiny micro tears in the muscles that are being used. The body then, miraculously, begins to rebuild itself, to fix these tears. It needs building material to do so in the form of food. Food is broken down by the body to provide the material, but it needs good quality food, which is to say as good quality building material. Simply put, good material provides for a solid reconstruction, while poor material means not such a quality rebuild—or even a breakdown of the body over time.

It's during rest time that the body then uses the food to restore the body, and it's during rest that the body uses the food to rebuild the body stronger. It will come back stronger when it has both quality building material and quality rest to do so.

This is, in my opinion, why some athletes at the height of their career—or people exercising for fitness—may crash and burn. They may have eaten high calorie, low quality food. They did not pay attention to providing the body with adequate nourishment—that is, quality foods that are highly nutritious and nutrient-dense, as well as quality rest, and restorative time.

I know this first hand. At the onset of my running life, I did eat the high calorie foods like ice cream. As you know, ice cream is high in calories, not high in nutrients.

I was running to mostly lose weight or be able to eat whatever I wanted without gaining weight. I ate just enough calories to maintain this. The problem was, because ice cream has such little nutrient value, I was starting to run my body down. I wasn't getting the benefits of exercise: increased energy, vitality, and muscle development. I was growing tired, irritable, and not sleeping so well—as well as experiencing some aches and pains in my joints. I was tired walking up stairs. I was not so enthused about going out for a run.

Then, I began to gain weight! All because I was not eating nutritious food nor getting adequate rest. My sleep was poor due to all the sugar, bars and gels I was consuming. It was a double whammy of not nourishing an active body.

Of course, then the cycle begins: gain weight, exercise more, limit calorie intake, metabolism slows down, gain more weight, exercise more, and so on. Those of you who have done this know what I mean. It's a cycle. We can feel so crappy, yet not let ourselves do the things that are needed most—have nutritious food and rest! Nourishment for the body.

A Binge is a Binge: Healthy Food Included

Emotional eating is emotional eating, a binge is a binge, numbing to the present moment is numbing, even if you are choosing healthy food. As I became more aware that I was eating emotionally as a reaction to feeling stressed or experiencing strong, deep-rooted negative thoughts, I was still reacting by eating. But, I started to eat healthier foods, including when I was binging.

At first, I felt good about eating the healthier food. But then I realized—wait, this isn't any better. I still haven't gotten to the root of what's bothering me. Though I was eating healthy food, I was still emotionally reacting with eating. I hadn't really addressed why I was reacting, or really gotten to the root of what I was reacting to. I still reacted with food instead of acted. More insight came from this realization.

I am still feeling out of control. Funny though, I was now aware of what I was doing. I was stressed, I realized, and was dealing with it by eating a salad instead of a bag of chips. It was this awareness that then lead me to stop—most of the time.

This new awareness of the fact that I was still reacting to stress by choosing to eat healthier food lead me to realize I had more work to do. It wasn't about the food. It was about the stress, the emotions, the anxiety that I wanted to (needed to) address. It was about getting clearer of my own behavior.

Intuition: Trusting the Body, Again

Contrast—experiencing what we don't want helps us *get clear on what we do want*. Maybe you've spent a few months, years, doing stuff you now realize you don't want or don't enjoy. No need to woefully regret time spent on want you don't want. Just realize that that time helped you get clear—as well as left s p a c e for you to have compassion for others who may have similar experiences to yours.

You can become a good teacher in that regard. During this time, you may have been taught not to trust your body; it was the enemy. But now, having read this book and taken steps, you realize—or are at least closer to understanding—the body has been the messenger all along. You had many good reasons to do what you did, most likely to survive. And slowly, you have learned to trust this magnificent machine to guide you once again.

Recovery may involve not necessarily asking the right question, but asking the question *the right way*. For example, how is this behavior serving me? What is the message, the wisdom, I can gain from this?

In the Name of Love! Part II

We cannot eat whatever we want, well we can but there can be consequences. But you can decide for yourself, choosing the experience you want to have based on what you eat. This is not the same as food rules. Food rules tell us what we can and cannot eat. I am talking about, from my experience, of letting my body tell me what to eat in the moment. You can eat all the sugar you want, but if done with or without awareness, or done ignoring the messages from the body, there are consequences.

Consequences such as low energy, irritability, or possibly in time develop type ll diabetes. The approach is not calories in, calories out, though I took that route for many years. This does not make for a healthy body in the long run. This is about body and mind awareness. What I did was to educate myself, to get back into *my body*, to trust it above all else, to let my body guide me, not rules, nor science, not my emotions. Now without rules, but with great awareness, could I then embrace this body and feed it food outta love. Life is an endurance sport, I feel it wise to prepare the body for this long event to make it a good one.

The bottom line, though, is to enjoy food and sport as life enhancers, for pleasure, to show reverence for this magnificent body you are in.

Take a few minutes each day to have a quiet, personal conversation with it! Listen to the body, not the mind. Sometimes I enjoy active meditation while walking, cycling, running, swimming, just about anything that involves getting outside.

When I wake up, I consider what I feel like doing and not think about it too much. Some days, I will sit and write. Other days, it's an active meditation with yoga or running. Still on other days, it's a few minutes of sitting meditation.

This all comes from a feeling, not a thought. Ask yourself, "What do I feel pulled to go and do?" Start with a deep breath, always using the breathing to center the body. A deep belly breath to awaken the inner body.

Note how you are feeling. What do you need in this very moment? Are you feeling inspired to drink more water, bend and stretch, or get some fresh air? What foods might feel good in your body? Warm tea, something light, something warm? How is your body talking to you? How might it be whispering to you? What is it saying to you?

The more you get still, the more you will hear. The more you hear, the more you will be guided. You will be more attuned to what *you* need. You can then respond to these messages that work for you in the moment. You don't need to go outside of yourself for guidance, answers. They are all there for you.

Today I feel puffy

Today I feel puffy, fat, my clothes don't seem to fit so well. Sound familiar? Funny—yesterday, I felt fit and skinny. How could I have changed so much in less than a day? Through my awareness, by paying attention, I came to this realization: Of course I did *feel* fat, but what I realized is what I felt or what I needed *was rest*.

My wonderful body was telling me something: rest. But, my mind was up to its old habitual shenanigans, which I fortunately did not listen to. While my body was sending signs to rest, my mind hit the "play" button of the old tape that said: You are fat. How could you have been so stupid yesterday to think you weren't? Here you are today. Clothes are tight. Why expect anything different. Whew! The ego can be exhausting at times, and it can flip "on" quickly as though you just hit a light switch!

The mental struggles for me was to *know* my body was swollen from the training, which does happen, can happen post exercise as the body attempts to heal, recover and grow stronger from the effort. As soon as I allowed myself the needed rest, my body reacted well. The swelling went down and I once again felt healthy, strong, and fit.

Stillness Now

Noticing stillness now as I write, beautiful among these mountains, I feel I am most at home in nature. I escaped into the mountains back in 1989. Getting out of the city by retreating to the mountains, to "lick my wounds," I as used to refer to it, to heal. I realized I was not a city person. I needed and wanted to immerse myself in nature where I felt most at peace, most connected to me. I healed myself from discord by swimming in the mountain lakes, hiking to the top of the peaks, running and biking the roads and trails, and staring at the sunsets each evening and the stars at night. I needed, wanted the quiet, the stillness of the mountains

Eventually, I discovered triathlon and I was hooked after my first race. At first, it was pure love doing triathlon. I was combining all that I love doing into one day, one event. I had done many years of running races, but this was all new. I loved doing outdoor activities and always felt my best when outside—appreciating the beauty all around me. Triathlon was a perfect for me as I felt I was a person who couldn't commit to one sport. It was the sport for people who couldn't decide which sport they liked best, so I did all three!

Eventually doing triathlons became a love and fear combined. It was a time when the truth about myself emerged. Here, I recognized my negative voice - *I have to do more, I'm never satisfied* - and I totally attached my value to the outcome of my training and racing.

I had a chance to listen, given all the hours spent alone during training. I had to recognize my true feelings at one point or quit the sport. My "never good enough" mentality meant I was driving myself insane. But even if I quit triathlon, I realized that I would still be swimming, biking and running. I do love these activities, so I would never stop. Finally, I discovered I was much happier when I removed the competitive piece, when not training by script, but instead I was free-wheeling it on my own.

What I would do is write a schedule each week. I'd do whatever seemed fun and felt like a pull to do. I found out the more I heeded my inner pull, the more I enjoyed the workout, the more fun I had, and the better I felt. The more enjoyable the workouts were, leading up to a race, the better my performance on race day. You cannot have a happy ending if the journey has not been a pleasant one, I discovered. Over the years, I had worked with a few different triathlon coaches with good success on race day, but I didn't enjoy the journey so much. I didn't like structure associated with the training; I felt too much in a box.

The last time I had a triathlon coach was for the Half Ironman (a race that consists of a 1.2 mile swim, 56 mile bike ride then a 13.1 mile run) World Championship in Florida. I had an excellent race at the age of 47, with the goal to get back to my best Half Ironman time of 5:05 when I was in my early thirties. I was serious. I worked hard in my preparations. I was thrilled with my results, having attained my goal time.

Post race, I thought: *That's nice.*

It felt good to attain my goal. But, I realized, I wasn't so accepting of the process, the training to get me there. I was happy overall with the experience ("thank you" to my awesome coach at the time) but realized this was no longer the experience I wanted to have. I used too much energy, mental energy, to get me through the necessary training sessions to get me to my goal time. I realized I would rather train, listen more to my body, to my inner pull, than the training *schedule*, and accept the results on race day as they are. I was no longer attached to the outcome on race day, but more of the *process* to get me there.

It came to me in all the hours out there alone on the bike, during the run, and with my head submerged in the stillness of the water on the swim. It seems contradictory that stillness came while I was moving, but it was the stillness of my mind.

Maybe I was chasing happiness, joy, peace— thinking it was out there in front of me. Until I looked back and saw it was behind me. It was when I slowed down, in my mind, that it caught up to me.

Food: Mental Conflict

My conflict with eating during training and racing in consuming the bars and gels. These are convenient foods for the sport, yet highly processed, which seems to be a contradiction. I think of sports/fitness to be about health—yet eating processed food is the opposite, I feel. Even if the ingredients of the bars and gels are from whole food sources, it's still processed. I feel foods that are not processed are best. But, I acknowledge that the less processed food with more whole food ingredients is the lesser of two evils, as they say, when compared with highly processed foods. I choose this alternative when faced with a choice.

Yet my inner conflict is still that *these are still processed foods*. How good or healthy can this be for me if I am exercising and training, yet eating all of this processed food? And yet, this packaged food made it more convenient at times to race and train as it provided fuel for me.

This was a mental challenge. Would I need to change my perspective if racing was to remain part of my overall health routine? What to eat during training and racing and still feel healthy was on my mind. How could I avoid or limit these processed, questionable foods?

To satisfy my conflict, I chose to limit bars, gels, sugary drinks, and powdery drinks. I moved to shorter events, to accommodate my choice to reduce my intake of these processed energy products. As a result of this choice, I created my own "sport" drink for training and racing by combining water, pure maple syrup, lemon and salt. In place of the gels I discovered eating dates which I find are delicious and work well with my digestive system. Real food! Yum!

This mix worked for me, but more importantly, I felt better about ingesting it. However, the syrup is still sugar in the body, so I still feel that limiting it is wise, even if it is a non-processed source. The gels (I have stayed with one brand) I only use on race day. I have used the same brand and flavors for years, sticking with them. On race day, I won't limit myself with the calories my body needs.

I would like to point out that we all need to be aware of the overall big picture: How much processed foods are being consumed in the name of sport and the ease of using them?

I used to eat energy bars frequently, lots of them — too many of them. I'd eat them as a meal replacement or as a supplement or as a snack, and sometimes, like dessert. They are just so convenient! Some of them are so tasty; some of them are kind of heavy and dense. But regardless of convenience and taste, I eventually felt I would be better eating real food. I'd again think: *they are still a processed food?* I also realized I was missing the taste of whole food, as well as the micro nutrients that come along with it. Again, even if the source of the ingredients for the bar were from whole food, it had to be processed to make it into the bar and to lengthen the shelf life of it. Nutrients could be lost, and overall, again, wouldn't I just be better eating the whole food instead of the bar?

I also realized that eating so many bars had become a habit. I had gotten a little lazy about taking care of myself, by not leaving time to prepare meals to nourish myself. Instead, I was depending on the convenience of bars. I missed the taste of real food as well as feeling "normal" when eating real, whole food. The tradition of sitting down to eat a meal at a table, with plate and silverware (relaxed, as opposed to unwrapping a bar while mobile) was lacking. I was both emotionally and physically missing the "ceremony" of eating.

Soon enough, though, I noticed my body was craving real food—not bars, gels and powder drinks.

Yet, I feel it's easy to get pulled into the "sexy promise" of consuming these bars and drinks. There is such great marketing around these products for athletes, as though these products are the elixir of life for performance. The strong consistent message is that by consuming "x" product, it will make you strong, faster, more amazing. And that you "need" this product for *your best you*. We are all being pitched on this idea that we need this product to succeed, to reach the personal goal laid out there, and to be special.

At the same time, there is this underlying feeling that if you don't consume it, who knows what will happen? It's a little fear-based marketing that speaks to the ego in all of us, that gets to us when we are most vulnerable and not paying attention. These marketers are good. They speak to our emotions, and by golly, they can get us!

But, I ask, what about all those great athletes and their performances before these "must have" special products came about? What did they do, and what did they eat in order to maximize their outcome?

I can remember standing in front of the shelves of the "health food" section in the grocery store years ago when I was feeling poorly about myself. I recall my desperation to want to lose weight, to want to feel good and to just feel "normal."

The pull was so strong then—the wish, the desire to just be able to buy certain foods to solve all my problems. It was like this: If I could just get the right food, the right protein powder, the right cereal, or vitamin or supplement, I'd then lose weight, feel good, and finally have the life I was craving. I'd finally be happy!

At first, I literally bought into this, this idea, this stuff. After a while, though I wisened up. I now stand and listen to the thoughts running through my head—to understand what I am looking for in this or that container. *Why do I feel compelled to buy this powdery drink mix?* I ponder. What do I *really want* out of consuming this? What do I believe it will do for me by having it, taking it in? Such thoughts as this come to mind: *it will make me healthier, faster, more fit.* This container with all its promises tempts me. I think: *I will have these things because of this drink.* They are good those marketers, I think. My belief for a moment is that these experiences (health, speed, and fitness) are in this container of dry, chocolate flavored powder— which will quickly and easily provide all that *and more* for me. It's about the longing.

It is so seductive.

I finally recognize what I really want, what I am really looking for, as I stare at this container— innocently, yet seductively, vying for my emotional attention—what I want to experience *is not in this mix.* I leave the aisle empty-handed, sadly yet proudly I am not duped into this.

In the fresh produce section, I then pick-up whole foods—dark leafy greens, bright naturally colored fresh vegetables, and fragrant fruits instead. What I am really looking for comes from a little extra planning, preparation, and my precious time. What I am looking for comes from training, sweat, and effort. What I am looking for is outside in nature and my feeling on the inside that I am connected to it.

Fear of Food

For several years, I was afraid of food. I thought about it constantly: what I would eat, where I would get it, and how much I would or would not consume.

It was an obsession. It was a love-hate relationship. I can recall being afraid to be around food. At parties or social gatherings with a food table, I would be solely focused on that table of food, not the people around me. It was about the food and not the reason we had gathered. I ate food I didn't really like. I just ate because it was food. Oftentimes, it wasn't really very good tasting either. I would pick at food here and there—which felt a little stressful, not a very relaxing way to eat.

I also avoided real food, like a sandwich, for a long time, because I was too concerned about the calories. Two things happened. If I ate something I felt I "shouldn't" have (like cookies), I ate way too many cookies because I felt guilty eating them—and therefore, ate more, *beyond full*. Plus, I didn't enjoy them since there was a feeling of guilt. I say, "There are more calories in the guilt" and because of this eating more I didn't or couldn't enjoy them. Then there were times I was so busy *trying to avoid* the "not good for me food" (like cookies or ice cream) that I ate twice as much *in my attempt to avoid.*

Seems a little crazy, but it was my way of figuring out how to take care of myself when it came to eating. We all have to eat to keep ourselves alive, to keep the body functioning. But my obsession with food wasn't so much about the food as it was about using it for protection—or a means to avoid other aspects of my life. It was indeed a life preserver, but I would have to figure out how to get back to land, how to save myself so I wouldn't have to cling to it forever. Metaphorically, I'd have to build my own boat first, *then steer it to my best life.*

Eating From the Heart

It's so confusing what to eat these days. So much so that I feel there must be some conspiracy theory out there around what to eat. There are so many mixed messages about what's good for us, and those messages are forever changing, as well as contradictory. Regardless of what's popular, what's

the miracle food of the moment, or what's supposed to be good for us, I feel it's extremely important *to eat with love.* That is to choose foods out of love for the self and not based on fear. Fear meaning when our choices of what to eat are based on fear of getting sick, fear of getting fat, fear of being unhealthy. That fear is just adding more stress, more anxiety, more disconnect.

I now realize the value of making choices based on loving the self—that what we eat is an act of kindness and respect for the body, your life. Not only does eating quality, nourishing, tasty food fuel the body, it also fuels the soul. By showing respect and kindness for the body we are in—by choosing foods that feel good in the body and keep it running smoothly—we send a deeper message to the self, which is: *I care*.

EVOLUTION

"Once you make a decision, the Universe conspires to make it happen."
Ralph Waldo Emerson

Contrast

The first time I flew on an airplane was to visit a cousin in Florida. I was in my mid-twenties then, and it was my first-ever vacation. My goal was to be outside and on the beaches as much as possible. Day one, I was so excited to get outside on this beautiful sunny day. My cousin was not at all as enthused as I was. I said something to the effect of: "Let's go outside and do something. It's such a nice day out!" Then I distinctly remember him saying to me flatly, "It's sunny out every day."

Nothing like a gray rainy day to help one appreciate those sunny days. Contrast.

How easy it is to fall into the pattern of thinking that this is "good" and this is "bad." Of course we think sunny days are good and rainy days are bad. But we need *contrast* to recognize what we enjoy, appreciate, and to be grateful for it. Contrast.

Aren't rainy days great?—an excuse to stay home and read for a few hours, or take a luxurious Saturday afternoon nap! How nice to experience variety in all of life.

The Sun Is Shining Wherever I Am

One gray winter day I was skiing down the slopes of Cannon Mountain Ski area in Franconia Notch. As I passed near the chair lift, I stopped and looked up to the lift. I noticed an acquaintance of mine riding up the chair. I commented on the gray day, wishing for the sun to come out. His reply, the best ever, was: "Celeste, the sun is shining wherever you are!"

How true. The sun is out, all the time, if we perceive it that way in our attitude, with gratitude, and acceptance.

Trust

None of this awareness on my part would have happened, if I hadn't dissolved the structures or belief system in my mind, become aware of my thoughts, and worked to see how these two experiences led to my reactions and actions. I had to recognize and become aware of how my beliefs and thoughts were giving me what I was getting—and how in many cases, it was the root of my mind made misery. By leaving behind how I *think* life is supposed to be (structures/beliefs) I was able to *feel* my way through my day, my life. I was able to be, and to do, as I needed in the moment at hand. I could trust myself and not *need* a structure to tell me what to do. I could decide what's right for me.

My thoughts and structures were at the root of my stress, anxiety, and fears—all of which I was reacting to by using food to compulsively stuff these feelings down. Instead of addressing the anxiety, for example, I was addressing my poor attempt at managing the anxiety with food. However, it wasn't about the food. It was about the anxiety—my perception, my interpretation of those feelings—that led me to eat instead of looking at the underlying cause of it all.

What I needed was less anxiety and better self- help tools for living, not food, to take care of or manage myself when I was experiencing the anxiety. This awareness has lead me to choose and lead a simple lifestyle by not filling my days with lots of responsibilities—overcommitting myself—and by living in the mountains in a small town close to nature. But, I do enjoy stepping into the busy world of the city and the travels I experience with my work. I embrace the places I travel to, the interesting people I meet, and the change of pace. However, I can step in and out of it. I take care of myself because I take my centered-ness with me, yet I am very happy to come back to the quiet stillness of the mountains, my home. I can step on the throttle of life and ease off it, too. It's up to me.

This I, *we*, must remember.

I allowed myself the time to step back. And what I found are creative, innovative ways to live that work for me, because what I thought I was supposed to do *wasn't working for me*. I wasn't living my authentic self. My body, my emotions were conveying this to me. I just had to let go, *to listen*.

Confidence

We are not encouraged to love ourselves. You may have heard such phrases as: "Don't get too big for your britches," and "Who do you think you are?" Or, "Don't be such a smarty pants." There are often well- meaning but misguided people, parents, adults, teachers, coaches, etc. who think they are protecting us from being hurt in some way by telling us these things. Most likely, they were told the same things at some point in their lives, so they're now passing this or that lesson along, especially to the little ones.

Yet we all know a deeper truth—that loving ourselves is our true nature. We then spend a good part of our later life "reminding" ourselves of our magnificence. We begin to listen less to the egoic voice as we age and more to our spiritual voice, following more our intuition. We judge ourselves less, and therefore judge others less. Without judgment, we accept ourselves more, and we start to love ourselves once again unconditionally.

We are here to create. We really do get to choose what we create. We also get to choose how we perceive what we create. We want the experience of what it's like to be *in the physical world as spiritual beings*. We are human beings, not human doings, yet we are here to "do." In the doing, we are not better than or less than. There is no judgment of how much we do or don't do, or what we do or don't do. We are all equal in the realm of *being-ness*. It's up to us to create, then live, our own experience as we wish to live it and perceive it.

Once you have "tried on" living in judgment of your body, you are always free to choose something different. Contrast. You may realize after trying to live with judgment or you actually experience living with judgment for years, that you'd like to choose differently—having non-judgment, acceptance.

You can trust yourself. You *can* have your own back. You will not judge or condemn yourself, and if you do, you easily let go of that judgment for you know that you are much, much more than words. You "know" at your core *that you are enough*—as you are at the start of each day and at the end of each day— regardless of what you "do" with the hours between. This is step One: awareness.

What I keep coming back to from all my experiences is: Step Two, which is to love yourself unconditionally regardless of what you do, or have not done. Know that you are enough without the doing. Step Three, we are all here to create, to live out truth. Each of us has a job to know our own truth, amazingness, and then live it, experience as we see it. There are no realities in this world, only perceptions.

Step Four: loving yourself comes with acceptance of all and everything. Add to this the healthy love and awareness you have for your mind, body, and spirit— which you show through the highest thoughts, the grandest words, and the most noble deeds that come from trusting your truest source, knowing all is well just as it is.

From this place, as you have taken each step toward love, *as you evolve from the inside*, the outside will change to reflect your inner world.

You see, health is so much more than food. Inner Peace. Grace. Acceptance.

Oh, One More Thing

What I am saying is this: Wake up, World! This is a book about a way of life. Actively Notice your World, our World. Start with your breath. What I mean by this: *feel* your breath. I know you know on an intellectual level you are breathing, but my hope for you is to *feel your breath*. Feel it now. Breathing is in the now. If *you* feel it *now*, you will experience life perhaps for the first time.

Stop talking and start listening with all your senses.

"Make a way for yourself inside yourself"
Rumi

56312919R00089

Made in the USA
Charleston, SC
16 May 2016